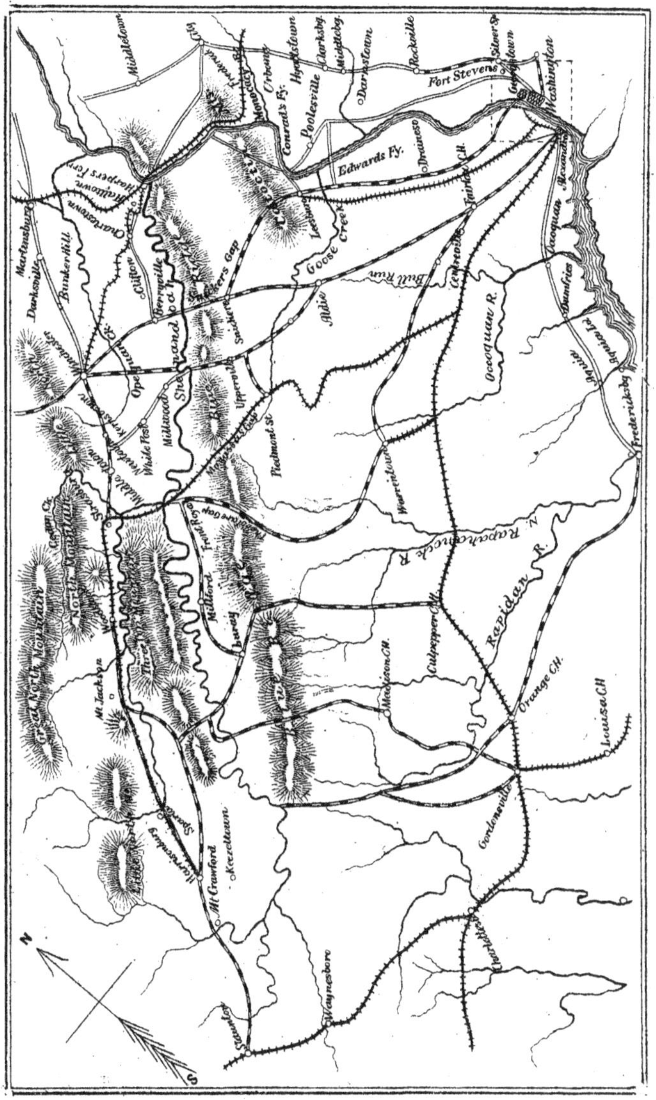
N
S
Washington
Georgetown
Fort Stevens
Rockville
Darnestown
Poolesville
Conrad's Fy.
Edwards Fy.
Goose Creek
Bull Run
Occoquan R.
Dumfries
Fredericksburg
Warrenton
Culpepper C.H.
Madison C.H.
Orange C.H.
Louisa C.H.
Gordonsville
Rapidan R.
N. Rappahannock R.
Waynesboro
Staunton
Mt Crawford
Harrisonburg
Mt Jackson
Great North Mountain
North Mountain
Luray
Front Royal
Piedmont St.
Millwood
White Post
Berryville
Snickers Gap
Aldie
Centreville
Fairfax C.H.
Bunker Hill
Darksville
Martinsburg
Charlestown
Harpers Ferry
Middletown

THE

VERMONT BRIGADE

IN THE

SHENANDOAH VALLEY.

1864.

BY ALDACE F. WALKER.

BURLINGTON, VT.
THE FREE PRESS ASSOCIATION.
1869.

Free Press Print, Burlington.

TO THE MEMORY

OF

THE MEMBERS OF

THE VERMONT BRIGADE,

WHO FELL

IN

THE VALLEY OF THE SHENANDOAH.

CONTENTS.

INTRODUCTION.

I. Preliminary.
II. Fort Stevens.
III. Snicker's Gap.
IV. Harper's Ferry.
V. Sheridan.
VI. To Strasburg and Back.
VII. Charlestown.
VIII. Camp Life and an Episode.
IX. Opequan.
X. Fisher's Hill.
XI. A Month of Campaigning.
XII. Cedar Creek.
XIII. Conclusion.

INTRODUCTION.

EVER since the termination of the late war for the Union, so honorable in its object, and so successful in its result, the citizens and citizen-soldiers of Vermont have hoped and expected that some one, among the many who are in every way competent for such a task, would gratify her people with a published record of the history of her regiments. It is a debt which they owe to the patriotism and self-sacrifice of their native State. Her boundaries are narrow, and the number of organizations which she maintained in the field was comparatively small—seventeen regiments of infantry, one of cavalry, three batteries of light artillery and three companies of sharpshooters, comprised the whole; but as these, with the exception of one three-months' regiment and five of nine-months' men, were constantly replenished with recruits, the number of enlistments was very large in proportion to the number of commands, reaching a total of thirty-four thousand two hundred and thirty-eight men. The admirable series of Annual Reports prepared by our efficient Adjutant and Inspector-General, Peter T. Washburn, contain a wonderfully pains-taking and accurate résumé of the bare facts of the military life, the date of enlistment and of discharge, the promotions, wounds, imprisonment, or death, of each one of those thirty-four thousand two hundred and thirty-eight, save only seventy-five, not finally accounted for. We may well be proud of those Reports, which have not been equalled in any State, though it is to be feared that our Commonwealth may, at some time, regret the too frugal distribution of them, for which our economical legislatures from year to year provided.

These Reports, in addition to the marvellously exact regimental rosters just mentioned, contain also official reports of most of the actions in which Vermont troops were engaged, furnished by the various commanding officers, and a clear, though concise, history of their operations during each year, prepared by the Adjutant-General himself.

But these official records, valuable as they are, comprise but a trifling part of what should be preserved from the history of those terrible years. The musty volumes of a town clerk's office, be they ever so minute in their details of births, marriages and deaths, of deeds and mortgages, of taxes and votes, give, after all, very little insight into the state of the community itself, when fifty years have passed. It is the daily life that we wish to recall, the thoughts, the feelings, the customs, the gossip—the various incidents of every description, that fill up the outlines, and make the difference between a chronological table and a history. All the corresponding detail of the march, the camp, and the battle, our soldiers should write out and preserve, while the precious memories are still vivid. Critics may carp at their literary deficiencies, but their fellow citizens will thank them cordially for anything that assists in perpetuating the remembrance of those days, when the people fought their earnest war to save their beloved country.

The elegant and vivid monograph of Lieutenant G. G. Benedict on "Vermont at Gettysburg," shows how interesting an actor can make those scenes appear of which he was a part. The only regret one feels in its perusal is in the thought that this is all that has hitherto been done in this direction by our soldiers.

With an experience of but twelve months of actual campaign service, the writer of these pages cannot, of course, attempt to execute such a general history of the Vermont troops as he feels should be, and still hopes will be, soon compiled; but no such volume having been, as yet, presented or promised, he ventures to ask, on behalf of his State, that it be quickly done, and meanwhile to add his mite by giving, as well as he is able, all that his qualifications will permit him to attempt, the history of six regiments for six months; fortunately for him, not the least noted regiments, and not the least interesting and exciting months.

But he must explain that he feels it to be hazardous for him to undertake even this comparatively trivial task, from the fact that the regiment to which he had the honor to belong, and which he had the honor to command at the battle of the Opequan, (the proudest recollection of his life,) was not, from the first, a member of the Vermont Brigade. In fact, his regiment was for a long time treated by the "Old Brigade" as an interloper, with no claim to any share of the honor so justly due to the veterans of the Peninsula and of Fredericksburg. This position and treatment were felt most humiliatingly by the 11th Vermont when it was first enrolled as a member of the Brigade, on the 15th of May, 1864, near Spottsylvania Court House. Originally enlisted as an infantry regiment, we had served under the title of the 1st Vermont Artillery, in the defences of Washington, for eighteen months previous to our being ordered to take the field. The regiments which had been constantly at the front were meanwhile jealous of our "soft thing," and the taunts with which we were greeted when finally ordered to the service for which we had enlisted, were certainly natural, and perhaps just. It was hard however, to be suspected of a liability to tarnish the fair fame of the Brigade. We too were from Vermont, and why should we be less brave than our former neighbors, whose noble deeds had long been our constant boast?

But by the time that the command had reached the Shenandoah Valley, by way of Spottsylvania, Cold Harbor, and Petersburg, it was our belief that this feeling was passing away, and that the "Old Brigade" was beginning to acknowledge itself cordially glad of the timely reinforcement. It is certain that, while deficient in the fighting experience which went so far in enabling a good soldier to accomplish the most with the least comparative danger, the 11th Vermont never, for an instant, showed any unsoldierly lack of bravery. The writer trusts that now, after the final campaigns, resulting in the capture of Petersburg and Lee, and the joint happy discharge of the Brigade, including his regiment, it will not be regarded as presumptuous for him to assume the rôle of Brigade historian for a portion of the period of his service as a member of it, even though his memoranda and his memory may be especially particular respecting his own command, while merely general concerning the other older regiments. No one honors the "old" regiments more than he, and he will do his best to be fair towards all. Meanwhile, if his own regiment seems to be made much of at the expense of any of the others, he asks that it be kindly considered in his favor that every man loves his own; that it cannot be otherwise than that he should have been especially impressed by its exploits which he saw, rather than by others equally worthy, of which he only heard, or, perhaps, of which he failed to hear; and that during the period under consideration the 11th actually constituted about one half of the entire Brigade; and having introduced this somewhat delicate subject, he cannot refrain from saying that, after a few months field experience, his regiment became again disposed to punctiliously insist on its full official designation of 1st Artillery 11th Vermont Volunteers, and its members gloried in their nickname of "Heavies."

A. F. W.

I.

PRELIMINARY.

The part taken in the late war by the Vermont Brigade can never be forgotten while thanks remain for any Northern soldiers. In the war for Independence the "Green Mountain Boys" made their name historic; in the war for the Union their descendants revived the ancestral glory, and earned new honor for their State. Without the assistance of the metropolitan press, without political influence, and under officers unknown to fame, this organization fairly fought its way into prominence and became the theme of universal praise. Citizens of the model Republic of our thirty-six Republican States, these soldiers might have been expected to do their duty always, and well. They added to that the exhibition of uniform and most unusual capacity to meet the emergencies of war, and a remarkable quality of steady quiet courage, comparison with which was the highest honor. If a good reputation was ever honestly earned, if any martial renown can ever stand the test of candid investigation, that reputation and that renown belong to the Vermont Brigade.

2

The consolidation of various regiments from the same State into one command, might, with profit to the service, have been carried much further than it was. Its success, in brigades formed solely from citizens of Wisconsin, Michigan, New Jersey and Vermont, was, in each instance, complete. It was urged against the plan that if it were generally pursued, some severe loss might chance to suddenly fall upon one community, which would be distributed among various States, if troops from different sections were commingled; and also that emulation within brigades would be promoted by uniting stranger regiments, from different parts of the country; but the result proved that the average mishaps were, on the whole, very evenly distributed throughout the army, and that the larger the command into which a spirit of unity could by any means be infused, the greater the good effect of the natural strife for excellence in competition with others. A leader's name, a past joint danger or success, sometimes produced this harmony; but the most ready and effective method, which was unfortunately too rarely adopted, was that which gave us the Vermont Brigade.

Memories of home were strong in every soldier's heart; personal acquaintances and friends of friends abounded in every regiment thus united; the honor of the State was felt to be at stake, in a higher degree, upon the deeds of the combined command; and when, as in our case, the organization comprised so proportionately large a portion of the entire offering of our Commonwealth for the three years' service, the effect of these state considerations became almost inconceivably strong.

It was notably recognized in the famous order of brave John Sedgwick, in the Wilderness: "Keep the column closed up, and put the Vermonters ahead!"

There was a "Second Vermont Brigade," consisting of five regiments of nine months' troops, which, under Stannard, did a marvellous feat at Gettysburg, their only battle-field. Their record is to be found elsewhere.

The Vermont Brigade was organized in 1862, and was then composed of the 2d, 3d, 4th, 5th and 6th regiments of Vermont Infantry Volunteers. Major General William F. Smith (Baldy Smith) was the original Colonel of the 3d, and for a long time commanded the Division to which this Brigade was assigned. Major General Brooks, who afterwards commanded the 10th Army Corps, was its schoolmaster; his stern discipline and lion-like bravery led it honorably through the Peninsular campaign, and the subsequent battles of Antietam and Fredericksburg.

While the Brigade was confronting Spottsylvania Court House, in May 1864, the 11th Vermont was added. This regiment at that time exceeded in numbers the entire Brigade it joined, which had just sacrificed its larger half in holding to the end, against Longstreet's repeated attacks, the celebrated plank road in the Wilderness. That wonderful feat of arms, which left one Vermont regiment but five officers, and another only three, out of over twenty in each when they crossed the Rapidan, gives a fair exhibition of the fighting quality of the Vermont Brigade.

The campaign in the Shenandoah Valley was the brightest period in our history. The men were generally well clothed and well cared for; the season and the country were alike delightful; the successes there obtained were palpable and complete. The battles of the Army of the Potomac had previously been terrible in carnage, and unsatisfactory in result; very rarely, if ever, had it witnessed the entire discomfiture of the enemy, and his confused retreat; and when, by the perseverance of Grant, Lee had, at last, been pushed to the wall at Petersburg, the very wall itself seemed a perfect barrier and a complete defence.

But under Sheridan all this was changed. The fighting was equally bitter, but we enjoyed on every occasion the unwonted excitement of entire and glorious success. The inspiration which that General gradually infused into his army, was unprecedented in our country's history; its fruit appeared long afterwards at Sailor's Creek, when two Divisions of the Sixth Corps unexpectedly seeing Sheridan leading their charge, broke forth into the wildest cheers, and captured Ewell with nine thousand men.

The Vermont Brigade, in July, 1864, was officially known as the Second Brigade, Second Division, Sixth Army Corps.

Major General Horatio G. Wright was the Corps commander, having recently succeeded the lamented Sedg.

wick, who had won in a remarkable degree the esteem and affection of his men, and who was rarely spoken of save as "Uncle John." It was a hard post to fill, and some quiet grumbling was, of course, occasionally heard; but General Wright, although sometimes unfortunate while holding independent command, was an exceedingly careful and pains-taking officer, prompt and energetic almost to excess; his great desire to be punctually ready, and to thoroughly accomplish the end of the moment, occasionally causing his men to think him unnecessarily severe. He was known among his superiors as a most admirable executive officer; first in the Department of the South, and afterwards as a Division commander under Sedgwick, and as a Corps commander under Meade and Sheridan, he did yeoman service for our cause.

Brigadier General George W. Getty, who was brevetted Major General in the Shenandoah campaign, commanded the Second Division. It may be said without hesitation, that the army did not contain a better Division General than he. True in all soldierly instincts; conspicuous for personal courage on the battle field; repeatedly wounded in action; careful in discipline, but uniformly kind and courteous to all; almost silent in general conversation; the impersonation of modesty; frequently overslaughed by men of much inferior worth, who, zealous for promotion, would condescend to fish for it in filthy waters,—but never complaining; intent on his duty, and forgetful of himself; a native of the District of Columbia, a West Point graduate, the husband of a Virginian, whose relatives at Staunton, in full sympathy with the enemy, were reached by our cavalry during Sheridan's campaign,—but with so many Southern associations, an earnest patriot; always to be found at the head of his men, who trusted in him implicitly; he was, all in all, the model of an educated American soldier gentleman.

Our Brigade was commanded by Brigadier General (subsequently Brevet Major General) Lewis A. Grant, a Vermont lawyer, who entered the service as Major of the 5th; whose bravery and whose energy were never questioned; who had, by diligent study, made himself so thoroughly acquainted with the red tape of the Regulations, that he became a martinet in his disposition to require the performance of many of its absurdities, which are especially ridiculous in a field campaign; but who, with all his fussiness, was entitled to great credit as a hard worker and a vigilant commander. The fact is that there is a love of minutiæ and a sense of the beauty of infinite detail, incorporated, by force of habit, into the very life of a regular officer, which few volunteers could appreciate, and which they were very much disposed to sneer at *sub rosâ*, while recognizing the great benefit derived, in time of war, from a corps of educated soldiers. For instance, a distinguished Division commander in the Sixth Corps, whom the writer lately accidentally met, joined enthusiastically in praising that organization, and said that it was acknowledged to be without a peer. My mind, of course, at once reverted to our brilliant battles and herculean marches, but he proceeded to explain. "General Hancock's Second Corps," said he, "was the only one that assumed to compete with us, and even he admitted to me, on the occasion of one of our reviews, that he could never get his artillery batteries to march with as perfect a line as ours did!" It was certainly the faintest basis one could imagine on which to found a claim for military preëminence, and the gravity and earnestness with which it was asserted, made it appear almost ludicrous. Such attention to trifles was esteemed by officers fresh from the careless life of the citizen, as certainly folly, almost scandal, in the time of our country's danger. We could, of course, value a clean gun and orderly accoutrements, while excellence in drill was willingly sought for and highly enjoyed by the volunteers; but a life spent in peaceful soldiering, where the only possible competition was in such matters as the comparative brilliancy of brass shoulder-scales, or the dressing of the ranks of half-a-dozen parallel six-horse teams, had inspired the officers of our regular army with a veneration for such nonsense, which tended greatly and unjustly to lower our estimation of their military capacity. They could fight too, and they proved it.

Now General L. A. Grant was constitutionally a Regular in such matters, without a Regular's experience and power of adaptation. This explanation may serve to make clear that the reputation for old-maidishness which he acquired among his troops, would, by many, be regarded as the highest compliment. On the battle field, the care with which he always provided for a skirmish line in his front, was especially noticeable, and though his Brigade was sometimes overwhelmed, it was never surprised.

The commanding officers of the various regiments were as follows: of the 2d, which was a "veteran" regiment, the three years of its first enlistment having expired, Lieutenant Colonel (afterwards Colonel) Amasa S. Tracy; of the 3d, Colonel Thomas O. Seaver; of the 4th, Colonel (since Brevet Brigadier General) George P. Foster; of the 5th, Captain Eugene A. Hamilton, this regiment having lost all its field officers in the preceding campaign; of the 6th, Lieutenant Colonel Oscar A. Hale; and of the 11th, Lieutenant Colonel George E. Chamberlain, its Colonel, (afterwards Brigadier General,) James M. Warner, having been shot through the neck at Spottsylvania, and appropriated by the Washington authorities on his reporting for duty, being assigned to the command of a Brigade in the northern defences of that city. This regiment, the 11th, on account of its comparatively large size served in two battalions, which were manœuvred as independent regiments, though usually side by side, commanded respectively by Major (afterwards Colonel) Charles Hunsdon, and Major (subsequently Lieutenant Colonel) Aldace F. Walker.

Of the men composing the regiments thus commanded, little need now be said. Their actions will speak for them as this account proceeds. Gen. Sheridan insists on every occasion that it was the private soldiers who fought the war: certainly whatever credit the officers of the Vermont Brigade attained was little, in comparison with the glory earned by the rank and file.

Its officers and men were almost all native-born Vermonters. Love of country gave it zeal, and the strength of the hills filled it with might. Its foreign admixture was very small; a few Irishmen, nature's cosmopolitans, and a few Canadians lured from over the border by the enormous bounties offered for recruits, were all. And in every soldierly quality no class of men is equal to the intelligent, reading, property-holding citizen, who wears his uniform to show his convictions, and uses his good sense in performing his daily duty.

An apparent paradox appeared which has been so generally noticed that it may be set down as one of the striking lessons of the war; the more cultured, refined and delicately nurtured the soldier had been at home, the better he seemed to endure the hardships of the campaign. The scholar would almost invariably outwear the laborer. And these soldiers to a man were scholarly enough to understand their errand and to know that individual duty done was the surest earnest of the peace they longed for.

Among their associates in the Corps, our Brigade was held in the highest estimation. The writer remembers that while walking the midnight rounds of our Petersburg picquet line one frosty night, he stopped to warm himself for a moment at an outpost fire. The five veterans on duty there were keeping themselves awake by reminding each other of this and that reminiscence of the past four years, and as some unusually vivid recollection was suggested, one exclaimed with the emphatic approval of the balance of the group, "Then's when we wanted the Vermonters!"

In claiming such a character and reputation the Vermont Brigade does no injustice to other troops which fought at their side. Except in an occasional instance of striking inferiority, little distinction could be made among the regiments from the north as they successively became merged in the army; certainly no one ever supposed that soldiers from Vermont were intrinsically better soldiers than those from New Hampshire, or Massachusetts, or Wisconsin, or any other State, if native-born, but the Vermont Brigade, in being thus consolidated, had a better opportunity than was usual, so that its regiments soon became harmonious, reciprocally trustful in each other, confident in themselves, and were at last recognized throughout the Army of the Potomac as composing an organization to be uniformly spoken of with esteem, and even to be regarded with affection as an honor to the whole command.

On the march, if the pace was for any reason hurried, the surmise was a common one that "the Vermonters must be leading to-day," for their stride was tremendous. In camp they were always courteously treated by their neighbors, and were good neighbors themselves, though it must be allowed that the state of discipline exhibited by the Brigade on the march or in camp never approached very closely the Cromwellian ideal; in fact the regiments were organized somewhat on the town-meeting plan, and the men were rather deferred to on occasion by the officers; not that there was any especially noticeable laxity, there was too much good sense for that, but there was hardly the least rigidity, and camp-life on the whole was of the easiest possible description. It was on the battle-field that the Brigade gained its glory, and even then it did not excel in feats of unusual or surpassing brilliancy; the troops which most notably succeed in the charge are those whose natural courage is tempered and restrained by complete official control: the most remarkable charge of the Vermont Brigade might have proved a fiasco if the enemy had not been utterly demoralized by its disorderly impetuosity; the occasion referred to was on the morning of April 2, 1865, when the Sixth Corps executed what General Meade pronounced "the decisive movement of the campaign" against Petersburg, and when the Vermont Brigade, being the point of General Wright's well-driven wedge, broke the line of the enemy's fortifications with a rush so eager and so unrestrained that its ranks were re-formed only after miles of pursuit and hours of victory.

The distinguishing characteristic of this command, and the secret of its acknowledged preëminence on the battle-field, was its most remarkable tenacity. It was seldom if ever driven back by a direct assault, though it passed through a field experience second to none, and it presently became justly and most honorably known as always and entirely to be relied upon. Such steadiness in critical positions, perseverance against all odds, and inability to admit defeat were the sources of its renown. Years of fighting proved the paramount value of such qualities, and brilliancy was at last admitted on all hands to be less important and less serviceable than steady, persevering, confident pluck.

No description of the organization in which we served would be complete unless it mentioned the system of badges used to distinguish its subdivisions. The badge of the Sixth Corps was the simple Greek Cross, (see cover.) Flannel cloth for the purpose was issued by the Quartermaster's Department on the usual requisitions. This cloth, unless some more elaborate material was procured, was worn by every member of the different Divisions in the three national colors, First Division red, Second Division white, Third Division blue. Each General officer was followed by a mounted orderly bearing a headquarters flag which showed at a glance the command to which he was attached. Thus the Corps commander's flag was a white cross on a large blue pennant; the flags of the Division Generals were square,—of the First, a red cross on a white ground, of the Second, a white cross on a blue ground, and of the Third a blue cross on a white ground: while the Brigade commanders were attended by smaller triangular flags, each in the Second Division showing our white cross, and that of our second Brigade being upon a red ground. The flag we followed during the campaign of 1864 now hangs in the State House at Montpelier:

in less than six months it was in the thickest of the important battles at the Wilderness, Spottsylvania, Cold Harbor, Petersburg, Charlestown, the Opequan, Fisher's Hill, and Cedar Creek, besides a larger number of minor affairs in which the Brigade was engaged, the total number of Vermonters killed and wounded under its lead and during that brief period reaching the terrible aggregate of *three thousand one hundred and sixteen.*

II.

FORT STEVENS.

The Sixth Corps, for the first time detached from the Army of the Potomac, took ship at City Point on the 10th of July, 1864, (Col. Perley P. Pitkin, the first quartermaster of the Second Vermont, but at this time in charge of all the land and water transportation of General Meade's army, superintended the embarkation,) and reached Washington in the evening of the following day. It disembarked to the music of Early's artillery on the morning of the 12th, and promptly marched up Seventh Street through the city, and out the pike to the front. We found the citizens in a state of great and not surprising consternation. The cannon of the enemy, whose camp was only five miles north from the Capitol, had been heard continually for two days, and it was known that the works were insufficiently manned; a few green hundred-day regiments, the scrapings of the convalescent camps, and some civilian government clerks and employees hastily armed in the emergency, comprised the entire garrison of the sixteen miles of forts and works that encircled the city on the north of the Potomac. And the lines on the south of the river of equal extent had likewise to be occupied with the slender force at hand, although the rebels were not in force in that direction.

Therefore the sight of the Veterans of the Sixth Corps was an intense relief to the constitutionally timid Washingtonians. We passed through crowded streets; cheers, good wishes, and fervent God-speeds were heard on every side. Citizens ran through the lines with buckets of ice-water, for the morning was sultry; newspapers and eatables were handed into the column, and our welcome had a heartiness that showed how intense had been the fear.

We pushed on rapidly through the dust, and were soon at the threatened point, Fort Stevens, on the Rockville pike, a little west of the centre of the northern defences. This Fort, with two or three others in the vicinity, was in great measure constructed by the 11th Vermont, and just here that regiment had spent a year and a half of its military existence. Long practice had made its officers and men entirely familiar with the range and capacity of every gun, howitzer, and mortar, but they had the mortification of seeing the artillery entrusted to troops who could hardly load heavy ordnance with safety; when, by the lucky chance of its return to what seemed to it like home, great good might have been secured as the fruit of its early labors, unfortunately no use was made of the skill its members longed to exercise.

The Corps was kept concealed in a forest behind the lines, while a grand Council of War decided how the so timely reinforcements should be employed. President Lincoln, Secretary Stanton, General Halleck, General McCook, General Meigs, General Wright and others, had carefully discussed the situation and had differed materially as to whether a vigorous attack should be made by the entire corps, or whether the enemy's position should be first developed by a strong skirmish-line. The latter plan prevailed, and rather late in the afternoon the attacking party filed down the pike in front of the fort and rapidly deployed. Minute details of this affair cannot here be given, as the Vermont Brigade was not involved. The sally was made by General Bidwell's Third Brigade of our Division and a company of about seventy-five who were selected from the various regiments of the Division and attached to General Getty's headquarters as sharpshooters, under command of Captain Alexander M. Beattie of the Third Vermont.

The pseudo-soldiers who filled the trenches around the Fort were astounded at the temerity displayed by these war-worn veterans in going out before the breast-works, and benevolently volunteered most earnest words of caution. The enemy's skirmishers were at this time within six hundred yards of the Fort in strong force, and their bullets, which were plenty, were assisted by shell from artillery planted behind them.

In a few minutes all was over. Our brave men

charged handsomely, for they meant business and knew how it was done; the enemy after a bitter little contest fell back out of sight, leaving us to establish our picquets for the night where we would. The Vermont Brigade relieved the charging party for this purpose, and the dignitaries in the Fort returned to their homes, having witnessed as pretty and well conducted a little fight as was seen during the whole war. President Lincoln was present on General Wright's invitation, which he says he bitterly repented having given, when to his surprise it was accepted. The President persisted in standing on the parapet, though an officer was wounded by his side, and his danger was a source of great anxiety to the General, who at last suggested that he should have to remove him by force, an idea which seemed greatly to amuse Lincoln. He at last consented to stand on the banquette, looking over the parapet, but was under fire to the end of the action.

The object proposed in this affair was to make such a display of force as would convince Early that Washington did not propose to submit to be tamely captured, and to relieve our line from the annoyance of the enemy's sharpshooters. It succeeded even better than was hoped, since as its result the rebels abandoned the vicinity at once. That night Early rapidly retreated, and there can be no doubt that the arrival of the Sixth Corps, with its prompt offensive movement, was the immediate cause of his withdrawal from before the city he had so bombastically threatened to destroy. There can also be little doubt that he might have taken it on either of the two days he spent in its neighborhood before our arrival from Petersburg.

In this affair the Vermont Brigade lost one man killed and one wounded from the Third, one wounded from the Fifth, and three wounded from the Eleventh, all serving at the time in Captain Beattie's company of sharp-shooters. This company lost quite severely in driving the rebel marksmen out of a house near our lines, from which they had greatly annoyed the Fort, and which was riddled with bullets and cannon balls.

The total loss was about two hundred and fifty killed and wounded on each side. At one point half a mile from the Fort, where the enemy had thrown up a little entrenchment of earth and rails across the road, a large number of his dead were found, and the struggle there must have been quite severe. A large number of his wounded were left behind in the houses near Silver Spring, on his hasty retreat.

Our dead were afterwards carefully collected, and interred in a lot just in front of the Fort, purchased for a cemetery by the government. The battle-field is now one of the objects of interest to Washington sight-seers.

All this was in the District of Columbia, and it served to give the semi-rebels in that vicinity a practical taste of the horrors of war. Perhaps a dozen dwellings of well-to-do citizens were destroyed because they obstructed the range of our guns; one situated directly across the pike from the Fort, and the residence of a widow of strong southern proclivities, at whose table many officers of the 11th had boarded for months, was saved until the last moment, and finally necessarily burned on the day of the fight, the poor woman being allowed but twenty minutes in which to remove her household-gods before the application of the torch. Other dwellings not entirely destroyed were ruined in the fight; all the crops in the neighborhood were trodden down, and the bomb-proof in the Fort was filled for days with terrified women and children.

The most notable injury done by the enemy was the burning of the elegant mansion of Hon. Montgomery Blair, then Postmaster General, whose subsequent career shows him to be of a most forgiving disposition. The residence of his father, Hon. Francis P. Blair, Sr., called "Silver Spring," was the headquarters of Generals Early and Breckenridge, and was thoroughly overhauled; it was left in the utmost confusion, the always hospitable table bearing all the marks of a famous carousal.

A carte-de-visite of some Virginia beauty was there found in the side of a mirror, on the back of which had been pencilled the following: "Taken from a pilferer for old acquaintance sake with Miss Emma Mason, and left at 11 P. M. here by a Rebel officer who once knew her, and remained behind to prevent this house from being burned by stragglers, as was the neighboring one. 11 P. M. and no light. July 12, 1864."

The photograph was left where found, but it may never have reached the family, as the credit of the preservation of the house was given to General Breckenridge by the newspapers. The above shows how much he deserved it. He had not then become the "extinct volcano" he has recently dubbed himself.

III.

SNICKER'S GAP.

After their demonstration against the Capitol, the enemy made their way to the north-west, proposing to cross the Potomac near Poolesville, forty miles or so above Washington. We lost some time in order to be satisfied that Early had not gone to Baltimore, as the presence of a squad of rebel cavalry on the Washington branch of the Baltimore and Ohio railroad seemed to indicate, and then the Sixth Corps was ordered out in pursuit, of course too late to overtake more than the rear guard which Early left on the north side of the Potomac. For a few days General Wright was the commander in the field, being directed by General Grant to go outside the works with all the available force at the disposal of the Washington authorities, and to follow up the enemy until he was convinced that they had completed their raid and returned to Richmond; but when so convinced, to retrace his steps and re-embark for Petersburg. Wright's independent command lasted only a week, but our exertions for the next forty days were tremendous, and we accomplished apparently nothing. Marching almost constantly, frequently by night as well as by day, we nearly exhausted all our energies, while gaining no credit whatever for our wearisome struggles. The army knew no better than the country at large what it was doing so vigorously, and we have never even yet been able to entirely comprehend our mysterious manœuvres.

Of course it is not the writer's intention, or within his ability, to give a military criticism of the operations of the Army of which our Brigade formed a part, but its services cannot be understood or narrated without continual reference to the general campaign, and the movements of the Army will frequently sufficiently describe the movements of the Brigade.

It is the more satisfactory thus to be compelled to touch upon the conduct of affairs at large, because the history of Sheridan's Valley campaign has never been even partially written, though well worthy the closest study as a continual daily exhibition of the highest military science: meanwhile the mazy period before the rising of his brilliant star must be hastily threaded through, although the task will be laborious and unprofitable except by way of contrast. We shall be enabled thus at least to see How not to do it, and How it was done.

It may here be said that but one newspaper correspondent fairly reported the movements and actions of this Army under either Wright, Hunter, or Sheridan;

Mr. Jerome B. Stillson of the *World*. A reprint of his letters would perhaps be as good a general history of these campaigns as could be given.

That first night's march from Washington, July 13, 1864, was one of the most fatiguing we ever performed. The Vermont Brigade was selected as rear guard to bring up the stragglers and the trains. The position occupied in a marching column makes a vast deal of difference in the ease with which the journey is performed: the head of the army, which always moves by the flank, or four abreast, being greatly preferable, for various reasons: chiefly because the obstructions continually met with from fences, bridges, fords, mud-holes, broken wagons, and a thousand other causes, compel the rear of a column to crowd up to a halt while the regiments which have passed advance steadily, so that the troops behind, as they successively surmount the difficulty, are compelled to make great exertions in order to properly close up the marching column; this alternate crowding and hurrying being excessively annoying as well as fatiguing. In order to distribute the inequality, the Divisions in our Corps always marched in numerical order, leading by turns; the Brigades in each Division followed the same rule, and also the regiments in each Brigade were each successively in advance for a day, the regiment, Brigade and Division, at the rear one day taking the lead on the next. The advantages of this system were so great that it was pursued even by the ambulances and the wagons of the trains.

On the march in question it was the luck of the

Vermont Brigade to be last of all, and orders were even received for it to follow the train. This was interpreted to mean that we should go in the fields or in the road itself on each side of the rearmost wagons, assisting them if necessary, and for ourselves, scrambling along as best we could.

Exhausted already with picquet duty for a night and a day, we got off about three o'clock P. M.; at nine we reached Fort Reno, having made in six hours less than three miles. Here we found Colonel Warner in command, and after a look at his headquarters and a hasty greeting, plunged forward through the Maryland woods and gullies into the darkness. The wagons soon became entangled, mired, and frequently upset. The mules and drivers were green, our old teams having been left at Petersburg. The road was narrow and of itself difficult. The men presently began to steal out of the columns and lie down to rest. Many were actually lost in the forests as we hurried on, and this horrid confusion continued all the night long. When we halted for breakfast we had marched 21 miles. The balance of the Division was then just ready to commence its next day's march, having rested for hours, and after barely time for a cup of coffee we struggled forward under the July sun, our system of rotation then placing us in advance of all. That afternoon we reached Poolesville, the last few miles of our journey being enlivened by the cannonading of a section of artillery, which, with a little cavalry as our advance guard, was driving the rear of the enemy toward the river.

Having thus marched forty miles in twenty-four hours, we lay still the next day (the 15th) near Poolesville, grumbling because our haste had been apparently so profitless. Here the 3d Regiment, with Colonel Seaver, left the Brigade, their three years' service being completed : a command of respectable size, 483 officers and men, (218 on duty,) under Lieutenant Colonel (afterwards Colonel) Horace W. Floyd, remained however, composed of men who had re-enlisted and who had joined the regiment as recruits, still known as the 3d Vermont.

On the 16th of July we crossed the Potomac at Conrad's Ferry; our skirmishers in advance driving a few rebel videttes up the hills on the southern bank, and our artillery shelling them as they galloped away. On our way to the river we passed through a corn-field already so high that the tassels waved against the shoulders of the horsemen.

The scene at the ford was new and exhilarating ; the river is quite wide at this point and about thigh deep : the horses were loaded double or treble, and most of the footmen, not having the fear of women before their eyes, carried their clothing upon their shoulders ; brigades were crossing in several places for a mile up and down the river ; every one greeted the unusual sensation of the slippery rocks and the gurgling water with shouts and laughter ; the burdened men were here and there overthrown by the swift current, and occasionally one would slip from a staggering horse and be burried for an instant in the stream, to the intense amusement of all but the unfortunate: in such a gleeful humor we re-entered Virginia, and laid ourselves out to dry upon her sacred soil.

Presently we went on through Leesburg, perhaps fifteen miles beyond the river, to the summit of the Catoctin Mountains, which we found to be a ridge of cultivated hills running north and south across the pike on which we were moving towards Winchester.

About this time General Wright's command, which had hitherto consisted only of the First and Second Divisions of his own Corps, was joined by his Third Division under Ricketts, just from Baltimore, by a Division of the Nineteenth Corps under Emory, fresh from New Orleans and the Red River, and by two small Divisions, commanded by Colonels, under Crook, which were known at headquarters as the Army of Western Virginia, but were incorrectly called by the rest of the army and the correspondents, the Eighth Corps; they were composed of Ohio and West Virginia troops which for a long time had served in this vicinity.

On the 17th Crook reached Snickersville, but failed to force the Gap bearing the same euphonious name; on the 18th the rest of the army followed, and the rebels crossed the mountain.

That day we obtained our first view of the celebrated Valley of the Shenandoah. Snicker's Gap, through which we passed, is really very little of a gap, being a slight depression where the pike crosses the Loudon Mountains, or the eastern Blue Ridge. We were marching towards the west, and were halted on a plateau about half way down the mountain on the western side. We thence for the first time overlooked a country with the topography of which we afterwards became entirely familiar: that beautiful Valley, the garden of Virginia. It extended north to the Maryland Heights across the Potomac, south as far as we could clearly see, and twenty miles or more in width to the western Blue Ridge, beyond the city of Winchester, whose spires we could perceive in the distance glistening on the plain. The surrounding country dotted with houses and groves and waving fields, well watered with wandering brooks, the fertile farms with harvests even then ripening in abundant promise, the occasional glimpses of the blue Shenandoah rushing past the very foot of the mountain, on the rugged side of which we stood, and the blue hills bounding the landscape where it faded into indistinctness, made up a most glorious view, scarcely equalled on the continent in its mellow beauty.

Meanwhile Crook, exploring across the river, had become entangled in what was called in the dialect of his troops, a right smart little fight; and though he was supported by Ricketts and assisted by sundry batteries on our side of the river, his men were driven back in intense disgust. It was generally understood however that we were under orders to discover but not to fight.

On the next day, the 19th, Wright finding the fords in our front commanded by the enemy, cast about towards Harper's Ferry to the north, or through Ashby's Gap to the south, for a circuitous route whereby he might enter the Valley with his army, the men meanwhile hunting for raspberries on the mountain side. On the morning of the 20th to our surprise Early was gone. The whole army at once forded the Shenandoah, or the Shining Door, as the soldiers atrociously called it, and moved westerly towards Berryville and Winchester. We went out three or four miles and found no enemy. Early had apparently returned in haste to Richmond; the cavalry could find no trace of his whereabouts.

That day every body robbed a bee-hive, and hard-tack was eaten with sweet-meats; ask the members of the Vermont Brigade for a list of the natural productions of the Shenandoah Valley, and every man will begin his answer with honey.

In the afternoon orders were decided upon and issued that changed the entire appearance of the game. Appearances indicated that Early had returned to Lee; our instructions were to see him fairly off in that direction, and then to anticipate him in reaching Petersburg if we could. All the General Officers coincided in the opinion that the object of the expedition was accomplished.

Crook's command was therefore sent on towards Winchester, being ordered to report to Hunter who had somehow turned up at Harper's Ferry in command of the Department, while the Sixth and Nineteenth Corps were ordered to return to Washington with all speed, where transports were awaiting us.

The conclusion that Early had abandoned the Valley seems to have been hastily reached, and perhaps was founded rather on what he was expected to do, than on actual information obtained concerning his movements. It will be remembered that we had been in full view of the rebel army on the previous evening.

But we faced about at once, reforded the wide and rapid stream, and with soaked shoes and dripping clothes began a long and tedious march. Blisters were raised on every foot in the first half mile up the mountain side. The road was a series of loose rough rocks, for weeks at a time in the rainy season the bed of a mountain torrent. Animals were suffering as well as men; many of them were shoe-less, and no forage whatever was issued for this campaign. It was midnight when we reached the summit. The descent was easier and more rapid. Faster and faster we hurried on; we came up with the Nineteenth Corps and went past it in the darkness while it was doing its Louisiana best. Thus we raced through Snickersville, across a ten mile valley, soldiers frequently asleep in the ranks, and the artillery crowding the road with the troops, past a little town where we had cheered so heartily, three days before, three children who saluted us with a miniature edition of the Stars and Stripes, the only Union flag we found in all Virginia save those we carried there; through a rugged region where every citizen was a guerilla, and our ranks were counted file by file as we passed, and where a few tired soldiers, unable to keep the pace, dropped to the rear and were instantly gobbled up and hurried to the Libby; till daylight found us once more at the western foot of the Catoctin. We climbed the mountain wearily, expecting every moment the order for the breakfast which we did not get, and went down its eastern slope still hungry, and kept on without any halt until we reached the village of Leesburg at nearly noon—a most extraordinary march whereby we hope that we helped to "save the country."

In the afternoon we went on a few miles further across Goose Creek, and the next day through Drainsville twenty-five miles further still. The picquet detail here found the memory of the Vermont Cavalry regiment distinct and pleasant in the recollection of the hospitable citizens. The third day (July 23d,) we re-crossed the Potomac at Chain Bridge and went into camp again in the northern defences of Washington. The 10th Vermont in Ricketts' Division which left Petersburg some time before us and joined us at Leesburg, claim, in the thirty days next preceding this, to have marched 600 miles, besides fighting the battle of the Monocacy. The Vermont Brigade in ten days had marched much faster and further than ever before, and had apparently nothing to show for it, except the unwelcome orders we expected on reaching Washington, for an immediate re-transportation to City Point, and the false information that the Shenandoah Valley was free.

IV.

HARPER'S FERRY.

Thus we obtained our first glimpse of the Valley of the Shenandoah, and it seemed probable that we should see it no more. But our departure for Petersburg was suspended, as reports were received that Early, instead of returning to Richmond, was again threatening Harper's Ferry and Martinsburg, having driven Crook out of Winchester with quite severe loss. We now spent three days in Washington waiting for developments. Meanwhile Colonel Warner at his urgent request was relieved from duty at Fort Reno and took command of his regiment, the 11th Vermont, which was at the same time detached from the Brigade, and assigned to the occupancy of eight forts, from Fort Stevens to Fort Lincoln, being those which it had formerly garrisoned. It performed garrison duty under these orders for one night, and on the 26th, was again ordered to report to the Sixth Corps on the Rockville Pike "for temporary duty" the order said, but the temporary part of it was soon forgotten. Meanwhile shoes and clothing had been issued to all the troops of the Corps, except this regiment which made the next campaign nearly barefoot; and the paymaster had visited the Brigade with the exception of the unfortunate Eleventh which was left penniless for four months longer.

On July 26th, the Corps was moving rapidly through Rockville on the road towards Frederick City; the Eleventh caught up with the Brigade on the 27th and camped at Hyattstown; on the 28th we forded the Monocacy, passed through Frederick and reached Jefferson beyond the South Mountain at 11 P. M.; and on the 29th we proceeded by Sandy Hook, along the banks of the Potomac and between the lofty mountains to Harper's Ferry, crossed the long pontoon bridge, climbed Bolivar Heights and at last went into camp near Halltown, four miles from the river and once more in the Shenandoah Valley. We were seventy-five miles from Washington by the route we had taken, and had made the distance in two days and twenty hours.

There is a very strong position where we rested, with which we afterwards became more familiar; a line of hills, descending to the south-west, extends across the angle formed by the intersection of the Potomac and the Shenandoah. Here we camped for a night, wondering in army dialect why this was thus. General Hunter was then in command with nearly the same army which Wright had taken to Snicker's Gap and there disbanded.

The next day, the 30th, we returned to Harper's Ferry and lay on Bolivar Heights, bleaching or burning rather in the sun, while we recalled the history of the celebrated village, and of the wonderful mountains which, on the North and the East, tower above it. We understood how basely Miles had surrendered his command in 1862 on account of a threatening occupation of the Loudon mountains by the enemy, even while his guns on Maryland Heights still fairly commanded the whole position. We saw the spot down by the canal where brave Colonel Stannard was discovered and recaptured, as he was attempting to quietly withdraw the 9th Vermont from the disgraceful scene. We gazed on the public buildings in ruins, and the sacked and riddled dwellings, with their mute sad story which needed no interpreter. And we remembered how the rash scheme of old John Brown, merely anticipating his time, had here thrown Virginia, mother of Presidents, into a paroxysm of fear, with its terrible combination of twenty negroes, five white men, and a cow.

Meanwhile Early had recrossed the Potomac above us towards Hagerstown, and on this same July 30th, Chambersburg in Pennsylvania was burned to ashes by the robber McCausland, who informed a clergyman there that "he was from hell," and doubtless told the truth. Our army was the sole defence of Baltimore and Washington, and must instantly be thrown between those cities and the threatening enemy.

Towards night we started back on onr weary route, halted for supper in Harper's Ferry; spent long hours in crowding troops and trains across the narrow bridge in the darkness, hardly making five miles all the night long, though vainly striving to make ever so little progress in the press of men and horses, wagons and guns, so that at daybreak we had our journey yet to perform. That Sabbath day's journey was the hardest march we ever made. The heat was intense; the day was the very hottest of all the season; the clouds of dust were actually blinding; the pace almost a gallop; the poor men struggled bravely, ambulances were crowded, shady spots covered with exhausted soldiers, men falling out of the ranks at every rod, overpowered with the heat and positively unable to proceed; actual cases of sunstroke by the score and by the hundred; a great scarcity of water; but no halt or chance for rest until towards night we reached Frederick City: that is, the mounted officers and the regimental colors, accompanied by from five to twenty of their respective regiments: it was straggling without precedent, or subsequent for that matter, but every man had done his best, and on the next day the ranks were full again.

After this effort Hunter remained quiet for a week, Early meanwhile foraging in Western Maryland and Southern Pennsylvania. The Sixth Corps shifted its camps once or twice for sanitary or other considerations, the last few days of rest being spent on the banks of the beautiful Monocacy.

Meanwhile the issues of clothing were completed; the weather became cooler; and, lounging in the shade, or bathing in the stream, we for the time forgot our hardships and enjoyed our lot.

V.

SHERIDAN.

On August 6th Lieutenant General Grant visited Major General Hunter at his headquarters near Monocacy Station. The interview was without ceremony or display, but it had an important object, for a special train from Baltimore arriving about 11 P. M. brought a new member to the council in the person of Major General, now Lieutenant General Philip H. Sheridan. The three officers went on to Harper's Ferry in the night; in the morning Grant and Hunter returned, and Sheridan assumed command of the Army. On the 8th, (the next day) he telegraphed to headquarters the result of a reconnoissance towards Berryville.

At this time every one is familiar with the career ot General Sheridan, but when he commenced the campaign in which he earned his first celebrity, he was almost as little known to the army as to the country at large. In the early years of the war he had been a Quartermaster, with aspirations to become a Major; afterwards a Colonel of Cavalry; then as a Brigadier he commanded an Infantry Division at Murfreesboro, Chickamauga and Chattanooga, where he attracted the attention of General Grant, who with his usual sagacity gave him the command of the Cavalry Corps of the Army of the Potomac with two stars on his shoulders. In May and

June 1864 he had handled his Corps bravely and well, had done some hard riding and some desperate fighting, but generally while detached from the rest of the army which knew little of his services except through the newspapers, and, in reading of them, made the usual Cavalry allowances. So that our army now welcomed his General Order No. 1 with no enthusiasm, and with almost entire indifference—in fact we were, on the other hand, a little afraid of him, for his only reputation hitherto was that of a desperate reckless fighter, and the immediate active campaign his arrival seemed to forebode was [anything but a pleasant anticipation. When he fought his first general engagement forty-three days from this time, we had learned that he knew more of war than simply the shedding of blood, and was a model of strategic caution as well as of decisive energy.

We did not then know the nature of the orders under which he was to act; they have since been published, and were to the effect that he must drive the enemy to the South and clear the Shenandoah Valley, leaving "nothing to invite the enemy to return." These orders were at last obeyed, though it was months before the end could be successfully accomplished, as the rebels were reinforced before we were able to bring on an engagement, and we were thus thrown on the defensive again. But there never was a defensive campaign so offensively conducted. The next month and a half was occupied in a rapid ceaseless game of fence with his antagonist, in which Sheridan though sometimes crowded, never lost the control, and which culminated after a final week of tantalizing thrusts at every side of the enemy's armor, in the terrible day at close quarters before Winchester, when after one of the most desperate struggles and admirable field-days of the war, the rebels fled from the lower Shenandoah in confusion, never to return.

In order to give a truer understanding of the campaign on which we were about to enter, a hasty estimate of the strength of the opposing armies will be given: Of Infantry we had three small Divisions in the Sixth Corps, which had already during the current year fought its way to Petersburg in the Army of the Potomac; one comparatively large Division of General Emory's Nineteenth Corps, with little field experience; and two fragmentary Divisions under Crook, well used to the work and the mountains. An extremely liberal estimate of these six Infantry Divisions would give them 4000 men each or 24,000 in all. We were soon afterwards joined by another Division of the Nineteenth Corps, 4000 men; and by two Divisions of Cavalry from Sheridan's old Corps under Merritt and Wilson, which with Averill's little Division already with us, were consolidated into a Cavalry Corps under Torbert. There were perhaps 8000 of these troopers, making 36,000 in the entire army. It was weakened however by safeguards, hospital attendants, teamsters and train guards, details and bummers of every imaginable description; so much so that it is very doubtful if at any time 30,000 men could have been found actually under arms. It was the great vice of the Northern Army that nearly or quite one-fifth must always be deducted from the paper strength "present for duty" in order to ascertain its actual fighting number; while the rebels, with far wiser economy, strenuously kept a musket in the hands of every practicable man.

At the time in question Early had four Divisions of Infantry, Rhodes', Gordon's, Ramseur's and Breckenridge's; the last was described in their newspapers as being, not as was erroneously reported, a Corps, but merely an unusually small Division of only 5000 men. At this estimate as the number in a representative Division, 20,000 will certainly be a reasonable estimate for the total of his foot. I have put the rebel Divisions but 1000 larger than our own, whereas they frequently contained four or five Brigades, while only two of Sheridan's Divisions comprised three Brigades—the rest having but two each. Early also had several unattached Brigades of Cavalry, and was reinforced about August 17th by two more Divisions, namely, Kershaw's and Fitz Lee's. On September 1st, after this addition, "Druid," the celebrated rebel correspondent of the *World* in Baltimore, gave a long and careful estimate of Early's strength, putting it at 35,000; it will be seen that allowing 5000 for his first allowance of Cavalry these figures are the same as those I have given, and Druid's estimate was made as small as possible for political reasons. We were probably the strongest in artillery, but our actual fighting strength did not exceed that of the enemy, if it equalled it. On September 3d, Sheridan says, "the difference of strength between the two opposing forces was but little," and a battle was then avoided until decided on by the Lieutenant General, after a personal inspection of the field.

On August 10th, however, before the arrival of Kershaw and Fitz Lee and before the remaining Division of the Nineteenth Corps had joined us, we were probably 6000 stronger than the enemy, an excess which certainly warranted a forward movement. With this view therefore General Sheridan at once concentrated his army before Harper's Ferry.

On this occasion our Brigade performed the journey from Monocacy in a train of cattle cars, waiting all night in the rain for our turn, but glad enough to escape the march. We took up our old position at Halltown until the arrival of cavalry from City Point, and the Sixth Corps with very good reason now began to call itself "Harper's Weekly."

VI.

TO STRASBURG AND BACK.

On the 10th of August the whole army moved out from Harper's Ferry and camped at Clifton, the name of a large plantation near Berryville. We marched, to our surprise, through the open forests and across the fields, scarcely seeing a wagon during the whole day. On the 11th we advanced, still diagonally across the country, as far as Newtown, leaving Winchester at our right. It was expected that the enemy would make a stand; we were therefore under orders to force the passage of the Opequan which covered their front, and bring on an engagement by striking for his right and rear. But he was too wary for that, slipping by us to the south. On the 12th we came up with him again at Cedar Creek, just beyond Middletown. These marches, though long and rapid, were made in most admirable order and with comparatively little fatigue. Our new commander was much complimented therefor, it being noticed that the columns did not interfere, and that the trains were made subordinate to the troops; but an order issued about this time by General Wright was of great value to his Corps. It prescribed ten minute halts every hour while on the march, with an hour for dinner at two, and a regular time for breakfast and for breaking camp; it also gave instructions to the various

Generals concerning marching distances between Brigades and Divisions, and contained directions in regard to various minor matters of little consequence in themselves, but uniformity and regularity in the performance of which added much to the ease of our journeyings. The only fault with the order was its two o'clock dinner, breakfast of course being at daybreak. The hour was however frequently anticipated if water was found earlier.

The Shenandoah Valley was also a far easier place in which to march than Eastern Virginia or Maryland. There was little dust in the roads, and moreover we were often able to march in the fields where the soft turf was a great relief to weary feet, and where frequent trees and groves shaded the columns from the sun. The supply of water was abundant, and the roads on which the trains moved were generally excellent, the turnpike from Winchester to Staunton, eighty miles, being probably the best macadamized road in the country; it accommodated two parallel columns of army wagons through its entire extent, while outside the fences on either side the frequent passing and re-passing of armies had worn bare two hard wide paths where marching had little discomfort.

Middletown is on the main turnpike between Winchester and Staunton, fifteen miles above Winchester and forty miles or more from the Potomac. It should be distinctly remembered that the Shenandoah runs north, forgetfulness of which fact has led to curious confusion in despatches as well as ideas; even General Sheridan telegraphed that he was pursuing the enemy "down" the Valley—towards the headwaters of the river. Below Middletown it flows close under the mountain at the very eastern side of the Valley, and is ten miles away from the pike. Just above Middletown the Massanuttan mountains, springing up abruptly, divide the Valley southward into two, the upper Shenandoah and the Luray, the latter being the eastern subdivision and the least important. Front Royal lies at the entrance of the Luray; Strasburg, two miles beyond the entrance of the upper Shenandoah, which debouches into the Shenandoah Valley proper midway between Strasburg and Middletown. Cedar Creek flows across the very mouth of the upper Valley. The ground is hilly on both sides of the Creek, and on its further side we now found Early's army.

Sheridan promptly sent over a skirmish line, which engaged the enemy in the usual desu'tory way. Skirmishing, as it became reduced to a science, depended on two general rules: every man must keep concealed as much as possible behind trees, logs, fences, buildings, or what not, and each party must run upon the approach of its opponent with anything like determination. If a skirmisher should show himself unnecessarily he stood a great chance of getting hit, and if he waited until the enemy came within forty or fifty yards, it was exceedingly dangerous either getting away or staying. The skirmish line was conducted on principles that looked to personal safety in a great degree, and was the favorite position of the experienced soldier. If however the holding of the position was essential, which was seldom the case, the men knew it intuitively, and the skirmish line required a battle line to drive it.

On the next morning, the 13th, the enemy had vanished, and the whole army crossed the creek to Strasburg. But that day's march was short, for he had fallen back but five miles and was in position at Fisher's Hill. This extraordinary natural fastness will be described subsequently. It is sufficient here to say that both from the reconnoisance made at this time, and from the examination of the stronghold after the battle of Fisher's Hill, every one was convinced that it would have been folly to attack it at the time in question, for an army holding it is more than doubled in strength. And Sheridan promptly came to that conclusion, falling back the same day to the camp of the morning on the northern side of Cedar Creek. Then followed a day or two of manœuvring with skirmishers and artillery, but no enemy appeared in force. At the time of a sharp little picquet fight on the 14th we thought the rebels were certainly coming; a subsequent advance by the whole skirmish line from right to left, made in splendid style in full view of the army, proved that no line of battle had as yet left the Hill. Two men from the Second Vermont were wounded in this affair.

Meanwhile the Cavalry Corps was watching the Luray at Port Royal, and on the 16th, Monday, it was desperately attacked by rebel cavalry and Kershaw's infantry. Torbert and Merritt held their ground and captured two hundred prisoners, from whom the fact was learned that Fitz Lee as well as Kershaw was in the Luray with two large Divisions fresh from Richmond, and that without doubt on the morrow they would force through our cavalry guard and plant themselves upon Sheridan's lines of supply. Mosby was also vigorously attacking our trains near Berryville, and rations were short already. The tables were turned like a grand transformation scene in a pantomime. Sheridan suddenly found himself in the most dangerous position of the whole campaign. He had been pursuing an inferior enemy and inviting a fight, but here was Early in both Valleys instead of one, with a force decidedly superior to our own, (Grover's Division of the Nineteenth Corps not yet having joined us,) and ten thousand rebels already on our flank, pushing for our rear; four days' rations ordered to last five, and great improbability about receiving any supplies on the sixth even; there was no more thought of pursuing a fleeing foe from the Valley, for we were nearly surrounded ourselves, and our capture entire confidently counted on by the enemy.

If we wished to escape from our predicament it was evident that we must run for it, and we did. The next morning, the 17th, we were the other side of Winchester, making the best possible time for our "base." The New Jersey Brigade and a few Cavalry faced about to see if any one was coming; in an hour they were scattered in all directions, the vigor with which they were pounced upon showing the disappointment felt by the enemy at the escape of the rest of us. On the 18th, at noon, we halted for "breakfast" near Clifton, and ate what remained of our rations—nothing in most cases—as the fifth day of the four was already passing. Then we resumed our march reaching the neighborhood of Charlestown at 10 P. M., being deluded all the afternoon by rumors that the supply train was only three miles ahead; we got a hearty supper at last, though a late one.

Ten miles from Harper's Ferry the whole army faced to the South in a good position, on our own ground at last. For the past two days officers and men had lived principally "on the country." It would not have been so bad living either, if we had not been in such a tremendous hurry, for green corn was then excellent and plenty, while flour and fruit abounded at the mills and about the houses. "Three days rations to last four" was always the order on the next advance, and the experience of the last two days had taught us how to obey the order without suffering, by merely using a little foresight. It was a hard system for the citizens, but yet severer measures were in store for them.

We spent the 19th and 20th quietly at Charlestown, the precise locality being designated as Welch's or Flowing Spring; a large harvest of guerrillas was meanwhile gathered in the vicinity; Sheridan had a barn full of them in rear of the Sixth Corps' headquarters. On the 21st an affair occurred which was only a skirmish, to the army at large, but which was inscribed upon the flags of the Vermont Brigade as the Battle of Charlestown.

VII.

CHARLESTOWN.

On the morning of August 21st, the Brigade was stationed at the edge of a wood two miles south-west from Charlestown. It happened to be quite near the picquet line, which described a grand curve around our left flank as it covered the army front perhaps half a mile from our camp; the ground the picquets occupied was undulating, and there being no high hills or prominent positions, they were posted on the crest of one of a series of rolling ridges in no way superior to others in its front.

The constant reconnoisances which our leader had indulged in for the last two weeks were a new sensation to both armies; Early now attempted the same method of getting information, but discovered nothing at all, scarcely any troops excepting our own Brigade being displayed on our side, though for a short time a general engagement seemed imminent.

The commencement of the skirmish was startling enough. While the army was making preparations for the usual Sunday morning inspection, the picquets suddenly broke out into a hasty fusillade, and then falling back in confusion were seen making rapidly for camp across the fields. Horses were hastily saddled, tents struck, knapsacks packed, and lines formed; General

Getty and his staff rode through our camp, and directed General Grant to move out at once and re-establish the picquet line. The order was simple, but its execution seemed likely to be difficult, for the line had been driven in for nearly or quite a mile in extent along the semi-circle of which our position was the centre, and whether by a line of battle or a skirmish line was entirely unknown, as well as in what direction we were to expect the strongest hostile force. Whatever was done must be done as an experiment; fortunately the disposition first directed by General Grant led to a successful result.

Without a moment's delay after receiving these orders, the Brigade filed out of the woods and into the fields in front of our left, in the direction of the heaviest fire; the Third, Fourth and part of the Sixth deployed as skirmishers and dashed forward rapidly, while the other regiments followed in line of battle more deliberately on various radii of the curve assumed by the skirmishers. Directly beyond the field in which we formed, there was a hill sloping towards us and covered by a large corn-field, of so high a growth that a man passing through it could not be seen; it soon appeared that it concealed a uniform line of rebel skirmishers extending over our entire front, and which had almost reached our camp itself. Our advance exchanged volleys with them, plunged recklessly into the waving corn, and disappeared. Presently the grey coats of the enemy were seen as they, retreating, clambered over the fence at the further side of the field and vanished beyond the hill. The rest of the Brigade excited by the success of the charge followed eagerly. The regiments on the right halted as they regained the summit of a second hill where the picquets had heretofore been posted, for the enemy in turn had re-formed on a similar ridge close in their front; but the regiments on the left continued to rush forward with more enthusiasm than discretion, until General Getty, who had feared such an excess of zeal and who in person closely followed the movement, succeeded in bringing them to a halt and ordered them back to the proper place. He afterwards told the writer that his orders were sadly disobeyed that morning: that he ordered the re-establishment of the picquet line, and before he could reach the troops on horseback they were half a mile beyond it, in the very face of Rhodes' Division drawn up in line of battle. The offence was of a nature easily forgiven, though the consequences might have been serious except for the personal exertions of General Getty, assisted by Colonel Hazard Stevens of his staff. The regiments had been simply directed to advance, the orders about re-establishing the picquet line not having been communicated to them from Brigade Headquarters.

As the left of the line withdrew to connect with the other regiments, the enemy in turn advanced firing heavily, and now a general musketry battle opened along the whole position. By this time all the Brigade had reached the front line, and, becoming deployed, covered the whole mile as skirmishers. The enemy attacked us from behind trees, ridges, fences, and walls with a force that could not clearly be made out, and with a vigor that expressed their disappointment at finding themselves no better off than in the early morning. But the Vermont Brigade, though pressed most dangerously, would not give way. The men hastily collected rails for feeble breastworks and scraped out hiding places in the sandy soil, being determined as they said to make a day of it. They recalled the skirmish near Funkstown in the Antietam campaign, when they had under very similar circumstances held a skirmish line successfully against repeated line-of-battle charges, and the experience of old campaigners was manifest in every action. The regiments at the extreme right were comparatively little annoyed and had excellent cover. The Sixth, about the centre of the line, was thrown well to the front owing to the contour of the ground, and the enemy got very near. It lost more than any regiment in the Brigade. One battalion of the Eleventh was well protected, while the other was in a position entirely exposed to the enemy's fire, the men lying in the grass by the side of a large brick house, and only able to get together a few rails for shelter, while the rebels from behind a stone wall at short range were annoying them terribly. It lost both its color bearers, Sergeant Daniel B. Field, who was instantly killed, and Sergeant John C. Pellett, besides many other men and officers. As might have been expected, Gen. Getty, whose horse had been shot while he was extricating the left of the Brigade from its previous predicament, came round on foot to inspect the situation, and as he was conversing with an officer on the loss of his favorite animal, a bullet whistled between the two; he merely interrupted his story to say in his quiet deliberate way, "That came pretty near you, Major!"

He now authorized us to occupy with sharpshooters the house above mentioned, known as the Packett House, and which had been hitherto under the care of a safeguard. Among the inmates were several young ladies, one of whom, tall and beautiful, dressed in mourning, and especially noticed for her bravery in the trying scenes that followed, was understood to be a daughter of Col. Washington, the vendor of Mount Vernon, who had been killed in the rebel service. These people were all at once notified to leave, and could then have done so with perfect safety, but they were overcome by the perversity of fear and could not be induced to go: though urged, reasoned with, and entreated, they insisted upon taking refuge in the cellar of the house. Still, as the fight was with musketry alone, there seemed to be no danger for them behind the heavy basement walls.

All the windows that faced the enemy were opened and filled with picked marksmen. The house at once became the focus of fire from the rebels in our front, and the troops on either side now had comparative rest, while there was a constant rattle of bullets against the walls of the mansion. Continual efforts were made to induce the owner of the premises and the women to retire to our camp, but in vain.

Presently, about noon, we were startled by the report

of a cannon, and a shell screamed over our heads. We understood at once that our position was a great annoyance to the enemy and that the missile was intended as a warning for us to withdraw. Of course this increased our determination to remain, and our answer was a vigorous volley from the windows. A second shell was tried with no better success. Again and again it was repeated, until finally the guns were depressed so low that one of the chimneys of the house was struck and fell with a terrible crash, the bricks flying in every direction. At this loud cheers were heard from the rebel lines; our only answer was still from the muzzles of our muskets. The eyes of all on both sides were now fixed on the mansion, as shell after shell plowed through its walls and exploded in its rooms. One hole torn in its side was used as a loophole by some brave fellow, not half a minute after the shell had entered, and the act was cheered vehemently by the soldiers without. Twice the interior of the house was set on fire, but the flames were extinguished by our men. Several shells reached the basement, fortunately exploding in different compartments from those occupied by the trembling citizens who now ran from the house to the rear weeping and shrieking. I have understood that the rebels, with their well-known tenderness, censured us for subjecting these females to such danger. It is certain, however, that our occupation of the house was absolutely necessary, and even decisive of the day's operations, and that everything in our power was done to save this family, well-known as rebels, from the weapons of their friends. None of them were injured. During this same season Lieutenant Edward B. Parker of the Eleventh Vermont was dragged down and actually killed by blood-hounds in South Carolina. If the southerners raise the question of comparative humanity they open a wide door.

At last after fourteen shells had struck the building and its front was spotted all over with the dents of rifle balls, a final death-bearing missile exploded in the very room occupied by most of our men, killing one and wounding others, strange to say the first that had been injured in the house. Hitherto in the excitement no one had thought of abandoning the position, but it was now seen to be prudent to do so; the order to evacuate was given, and the cannon troubled us no more.

But at once the musketry re-opened all along the line with renewed vigor, and the battle continued until the evening fell. Two mules were employed all day bringing up ammunition; the Brigade consumed 56,000 cartridges. So steady and constantly severe a fire has rarely been known; as the result we regained our lost position and held our ground successfully.

Another incident perhaps worth mentioning occurred that afternoon. About six o'clock a few of our officers were quietly lunching on the rear piazza of the shattered house from bread and milk and sweetmeats furnished by the owner who had returned thoroughly subdued, when their attention was called to a regiment from another Division passing out before the left of our line. Our men had no disposition to follow, though taunted with having spent the day fighting a phantom. The new comers marched boldly on, up a somewhat steep ascent, but preserving a capital front, until they approached the stone-wall mentioned above, when suddenly a grey line of rebels rose up, apparently two deep along the whole extent threatened, proving incontestibly that we had fought all day a full line of battle with artillery to boot, and had held our ground with a skirmish-line. Of course the valiant regiment which was to show Vermonters their folly, confronted by the unexpected apparition and saluted by a thousand rifles, fled in dismay without firing a gun, and we could not help greeting their discomfiture with peals of laughter, though the occasion might have been serious.

When the night had fallen,—and a very dark night it was,—we began to count our files and compute our losses. The Brigade suffered as follows:

REGIMENTS.	KILLED.	WOUNDED.	MISSING.	TOTAL.
2d,	5	11	0	16
3d,	3	15	1	19
4th,	1	10	0	11
5th,	2	1	0	6
6th,	7	31	1	39
11th,	5	27	0	32
Total,	23	98	2	123

Lieutenant-Colonel George E. Chamberlain of the Eleventh was shot through the abdomen, almost before the regiment was under fire, and while preparations were making for the first advance against the cornfield. He fell from his horse into the arms of Lieutenant Dodge, his adjutant, and survived but a few hours. Born in St. Johnsbury or its vicinity, a graduate of Dartmouth College and of Harvard Law School, he was at the commencement of the war in the successful practice of his profession at St. Louis. He entered the army under the most genuine moral compulsion—impelled by the force of principle and the feeling that he must do what he believed to be his duty, though very much against the wishes of his friends. His career as a soldier was what might have been expected from such antecedents. He was truly *sans peur et sans reproche.* Exaggeration is impossible in speaking of one who offered such remarkable talent upon his country's altar. Vermont should and will always cherish his memory as that of one of her noblest and bravest sons. While in command of Fort Totten near Washington he had married the sister of Adjutant, subsequently Colonel, Gardiner of the Fourteenth New Hampshire Regiment, a life-long friend. Colonel Gardiner was killed a few days after Col. Chamberlain, at the Battle of the Opequan, and the bride, a widow and bereaved of her only brother, an orphan before, was left in circumstances where sympathy alone remained to cheer her life.

Major Carlos W. Dwinell of the Sixth was also mortally wounded, and died on the 24th. He was born in Calais, Vermont, and entered the service from Glover, at the organization of his regiment, being then elected a Lieutenant. He was about twenty-six years of age at the time of his death, a farmer before he joined the army, and a quiet, pains-taking, valuable, officer. Though never thrusting himselt forward he was always a favorite in the regiment and the Brigade, and his loss was a severe one.

Lieutenant Colonel Oscar A. Hale of the Sixth was also wounded severely and subsequently resigned in consequence. The regiment was now left in command of Captain M. Warner Davis.

The army, having been effectually covered during the day by our efforts, marched towards Harper's Ferry as soon as it was dark, when the firing ceased. Our Brigade still held its place quietly, but every man was on the alert and recognized the danger of our situation. About 3 A. M. we received the long-expected order to withdraw, and without the slightest noise we stole away. Assembling near our morning's camp and marching rapidly, we came up with the rest of the army soon after daylight, finding them entrenched at Halltown, where they had spent the night spade in hand.

General Sheridan entered the lines behind us.

VIII.

CAMP LIFE: AND AN EPISODE.

We were now (Halltown, August 22d) in a position where an attack seemed impossible, and for a week we enjoyed our proximity to Harper's Ferry with its abundance of supplies. The cavalry meanwhile made daily reconnoisances by Brigades or Divisions, which the correspondents, on the watch for exciting news, dignified with the name of battles, leading the country to suppose that we were acting offensively rather than defensively.

On the morning of the 23d an order was received pulling us all out of bed and placing the whole army under arms at 3 A. M.; for a wonder it contained a reason for the unusual vigilance, a reason of surprising lucidity: to wit: "The enemy have been divided into two columns, part in our front." With perhaps too much precipitation we leaped to the conclusion that the other "part" was probably somewhere else: neither part made its appearance however, and we breakfasted in peace at daylight.

Finally Early, after having threatened to cross the Potomac at Williamsport, where Custer promptly met him, fell back from the river, and our army moved out to within feeling distance, taking its old position in front of Charlestown.

As we marched through that once celebrated village we found no traces of the gallows where John Brown swung, or the grave where his body is said to lie mouldering, but we remembered both, and our band, as did probably every northern band of music that ever passed there, reminded the rebellious citizens that "his soul" was still "marching on."

Torbert with the cavalry went out towards Bunker Hill: Early gathered up his army and struck at him. Sheridan, as usual present on the field, brought up Ricketts' Division and succeeded in developing the entire rebel line in the affair reported as the battle of Smithfield, with, however, little loss on either side.

Early now retired to the high ground west of the Opequan, lying on the pike between Winchester and Martinsburg where he held a long line facing east, while Sheridan got his army compactly together at Clifton facing west, his left near Berryville which Crook occupied after a severe skirmish on the 3d of September. The remaining Division of the Nineteenth Corps had now joined us *via* Snicker's Gap, and our force again equalled the enemy's.

The campaign as a defensive campaign was now evidently successfully ended. Early made no movement for a fortnight and our position was secure. Maryland was covered, while at the same time the enemy could not go to the south without our knowledge. The quiet was so general that we even began to talk of winter quarters. The rebels also appreciated our mastery of the situation. An officer's diary found on the field of the Opequan, under date of Sept. 10th, contained this entry, "The Yanks are just playing with us."

The cavalry however saw no peace, day or night. Hither and thither they scoured, over the whole adjacent country,—now creeping cautiously up in the evening twilight to the close vicinity of the rebel picquets, passing the long night with bridle rein tied to thumb and forbidden even to light the grateful pipe,—then at earliest dawn plunging at full gallop over the enemy's videttes and up to the very face of his battle line; or anon hunting the gaps and the forests behind us for Mosby and his partisans, who continually attempted to torment our rear and flank; guarding wagons to and from the Ferry or snatching up a convoy of the enemy's supplies from the Upper Valley, in sight of the rebel camp: the careful restless handling of those horsemen by our General, whose skill we now began to appreciate, has never been surpassed if ever equalled.

Our own Division also was in some degree an exception to the general quiet of the army. When we moved out to Clifton we were put in reserve near headquarters, and as a consequence we had all the extra work to do. For instance, on the night of Sept. 4th, the Vermont Brigade dug rifle-pits in the rain from sunset till dawn—not objecting in the least to earthworks, for we had learned to love them, and even Sheridan, the ideal of a field fighter, would as soon be without his ammunition wagons, as his entrenching tools; but it did seem rather hard, after painfully shoveling all through the long wet night, to march back to our old camp while strangers gleefully filed in behind our laboriously constructed breastworks. On another day the Second and Eleventh were sent back to Rippon to escort in the semi-periodical supply-train; and other similar errands occasionally varied the monotony of this long halt. On the 6th the Brigade held its shadow of a Vermont election: the votes were duly taken, counted and returned, the Eleventh, the only regiment whose figures the writer recorded, polling 237 votes for John Gregory Smith and 2 for his opponent, whoever he was.

We were now so far up the Valley that our supply-train as above suggested had to move with an escort; it came through once in about four days, usually starting on its return the same night; mail facilities were therefore limited, but a party of energetic newsboys reached camp every afternoon with the morning's "Baltimore *American*," perhaps obtaining immunity from capture by paying occasional toll in kind to the guerillas. About this time also a quantity of wall tents were received, the regiments being allowed one for each, for the use of the field officers, and a wagon being detailed from the Brigade Headquarters train for their transportation, the number of wagons allowed being at the same time reduced. Sheridan's own headquarters were always much the simplest in the army.

On the morning of the 13th, Getty's Division moved out towards the Opequan for a reconnoisance. The Vermont Brigade had the advance, the Third and Fourth being deployed in front as skirmishers. Sheridan and

Wright accompanied the column. At ten o'clock the skirmishers reached the Creek and crossed it at once, meeting the rebel picquets, however, but a short distance up the hill beyond. Capt. Cowen's Battery, going into position on an elevation on the hither side of the little stream, opened fire, the General hoping thus to discover the position of the enemy's camps in the vicinity, their strength, and other information of that nature. The Battery could be plainly seen from the opposite side; the skirmishers who had crossed were showing an occasional puff of smoke from their rifles, while the rest of the Division were massed in a wood, a quarter of a mile behind the artillery. The grove was clean and the shade was dense; the men were scattered in groups among the stacks of arms, chatting carelessly or playing their simple games.

The enemy presently planted a heavier Battery than Cowen's upon a hill on the opposite side of the creek and returned his fire; their first few shells, being fired at too high an elevation, passed over his guns at which they were aimed, ploughing through and exploding among the troops of the Division which lay concealed in the timber. Several were wounded, and the lines were formed for a removal to some other position, but it being noticed that the missiles began to fall short of us, we were soon convinced that our situation was unknown to the enemy, and in a few minutes the danger was over.

Among those who were wounded on this occasion was Lieutenant Henry E. Bedell of the Eleventh Vermont. He was a man of splendid physique, muscular and athletic, over six feet high, about twenty-eight years of age, a farmer, married, and the father of two or three children. An unexploded shell had crashed through his left leg above the knee, leaving flesh at either side, and a most ghastly mass of mangled muscles, shattered bones, and gushing arteries, between. As he lay upon the ground he he screamed continually, "Cord it! Cord it! Dont let me bleed to death!" The first rude tourniquet which a friend attempted to apply broke under the twisting of the ramrod, and allowed the spirting torrent again to flow. But when the compression was complete, he became quiet under the perhaps imaginary impression of temporary security, allowing himself to be lifted upon a stretcher and borne away to the surgeons and their ambulances without a groan. An operation was speedily performed. The leg was amputated at the upper third, everything being done for the sufferer that science and personal regard could suggest and the rude circumstances permitted.

Still there was very little hope. Though his natural vigor was in his favor, his very size and the muscular strength on which he had prided himself were against him, for it was computed that over sixty-four square inches of flesh were laid bare by the surgeon's knife. And it was also found that his right hand had been seriously injured, the bones of three fingers and of the middle hand being fractured and comminuted. The operation already performed had been so severe that it was thought best not to attempt the treatment of the hand until it was seen whether or not he would rally from the shock of the wounds and the amputation.

We returned to our camp about nightfall; the journey was a terrible trial to the wounded man. An ambulance under the most favorable circumstances is hardly a "downy bed of ease," and the jolting this remnant of a man for miles across the country, over fences and walls half torn down, and across ditches partially filled with rails, reduced the chances of his life to hardly one in a thousand, his immediate death being expected every moment. But, sustained by stimulants and his indomitable courage, at last in the darkness he reached the army lines alive.

Fortunately a house was accessible, and the use of a vacant room in its second story was obtained, where Bedell was placed on a tick hastily stuffed with straw and resting on the floor. And to the surprise of every one he survived the night; a little hope even of saving his life was awakened. On the second day after the skirmish the surgeons decided to attempt the re-habilitation of the shattered hand. A finger or two were removed, the broken bones were adjusted, and the patient rallied in good spirits from the second administration of chloroform and shock to the system.

But his struggle for life was only just commenced. After a few days of such rest as his miserable pallet could afford, orders were issued, in preparation for the coming Battle of the Opequan, that all sick and wounded should be at once removed to Harper's Ferry, twenty miles distant. Army wagons and ambulances were therefore loaded with the unfortunates, and an attempt was made to transport poor Bedell with the rest.

But although he had previously endured a rougher journey, it was while his wounds were, as wounds always are for the first few hours, partially benumbed, the nerves seeming paralyzed with the very rudeness of the injury. Now the torn flesh had become inflamed and was having its revenge.

At every motion of the ambulance he groaned fearfully, and it was soon apparent that to carry him a mile would cost him his life. He was returned to his straw utterly exhausted, all but expiring.

The army was to move the next morning. The surgeons were forced to decide at once what they would do with the dying man. In fact but one course was open, he must be abandoned to his fate. True, we were to leave him to the north of us, but in the Valley no attempt was ever made to cover the long line of our communications. Strong escorts guarded our supply trains, and for the rest Mosby had free swing. Moreover, though we did not know it at the time, Martinsburgh was thenceforth to be our base, instead of Harper's Ferry; and the vicinity of Berryville, where we then were, instead of being threaded once in four days by our caravans, as we expected, was not re-visited by our troops or trains for months. The wounded officer was therefore left on his chamber floor with a soldier nurse, and such hospital stores as he would be likely to need before his death.

We fought the battles of the Opequan and Fisher's Hill, "whirling" the enemy up the Valley, for a month supposing the Lieutenant dead. The attendant left with him followed us immediately; Bedell himself thought it best, and it was doubtless necessary, for the country swarmed with guerillas, and the system of bloody reprisals engaged in by Mosby and Custer reduced the probable life or death of the nurse to a simple question of time, had he remained.

It appears that the family who allowed our officer the use of the naked room as a place in which to die, were hardly pleased with their guest; in fact they seem to have been utterly destitute of sympathy, and to have thought it best for all concerned that he should leave this world and them as speedily as possible—and they left him at perfect liberty to do so. The promises they had so solemnly made us to give the wounded officer care and attention, were entirely neglected, and his chamber was never entered. Death, horrible in its loneliness and pain, would inevitably have come quickly, had not a Good Samaritan appeared. A Rebel among Rebels, there was a woman who most nobly proved herself to unite with a tender heart the rarest courage and perseverance beyond account.

Mrs. Bettie VanMetre was a Virginian, born in the Luray Valley, scarcely twenty at the time in question, and of attractive personal appearance. She had been educated in comfortable circumstances, and before the war her husband had been moderately wealthy, but now his farm was as barren as a desert, not a fence to be seen, and nothing to protect had any enclosure remained; there was a mill upon the premises, but the miller had gone to fight for his country, as he believed, and there was now no grain left in the country to be ground. Officers who had called at her door, remarked the brave attempt at cheerfulness which so manifestly struggled with her sorrow, and treated her grief with deference. For this delicately nurtured girl was living alone in the midst of war; battles had raged around her very dwelling; she was entirely at the mercy of those whom she had been taught to believe to be her deadly enemies, and who held her husband and brother prisoners in Fort Delaware, taken while fighting in the Confederate army, the brother being, until long after this time, supposed to be dead. Her only companion was a little girl, perhaps ten years of age, her neice. There this young woman and this child were waiting in their anxiety and desolation, waiting and praying for peace.

We should hardly expect the practice of active, laborious, gratuitous benevolence under such circumstances, but we shall see.

It is not known how Mrs. VanMetre learned that a Union officer was dying of wounds and neglect in the house of her neighbor, but no sooner had she made the discovery than all her womanly sympathy was aroused. As she would have longed to have her husband or her brother treated under similar circumstances, so she at once resolved to treat their foe. She would not be moved by the sneers and taunts which were sure to come, but she would have him at her own house and save him if she could.

The Lieutenant had now been entirely neglected for a day or two or longer; he had resigned himself to death, when this good woman entered his chamber and with kindly words called back his spirit from the mouth of the grave.

She had been allowed to keep an apology for a horse, so old and broken-winded and rheumatic that he was not worth stealing, and also a rickety wagon. With the assistance of a neighbor whose color permitted him to be humane, she carried the sufferer to her house, and at last he found himself in a clean and comfortable bed, his wounds washed and his bandages cleansed, and best of all, his wants anticipated by a gentle female tenderness that inspired him with sweet thoughts of his home, his family, and his life even yet perhaps to be regained.

The physician of the neighborhood, a kind old gentleman, was at once summoned from a distance of several miles, and uniting personal sympathy with professional zeal, he promised his daily attendance upon the invalid. The chance was still but a slender one, so much had been endured, and so little vigor remained, yet those two good people determined to expend their most earnest endeavors in the almost desperate attempt to save the life of an enemy.

And they succeeded. The details of convalescence are always uninteresting; it is enough to say that Bedell lay for many days wrestling with death, but at last he began to mend, and from that time his improvement was rapid. But although Mrs. VanMetre and the good Doctor were able to supply the Lieutenant's most pressing wants, still, much more than they could furnish was needed for the comfort of the invalid, and even for the proper treatment of his wounds. No stimulants could be obtained except the vilest apple-jack, and the necessity for them seemed absolute; no clothing was to be had, and he was still in his bloody garments of blue; delicate food was needed, but the impoverished Virginia larder had none but what was simple and coarse.

At Harper's Ferry, however, there was a depot of our Sanitary Commission, and stores in abundance. Some one must undertake a journey thither. It was a long day's ride to make the distance and return, and success was by no means assured even if the store-house could be reached. It was in the charge of strangers and enemies. The Lieutenant was too feeble to write, and even if he had been able to do so, there was no method of authenticating his signature. But a woman would be far more likely to succeed than a man, and in fact no man would be allowed to pass within the limits of the garrison encircling Harper's Ferry. So it came about that the feeble Rosinante, and the rattling wagon, and the brave-hearted solitary driver, made the dangerous journey, and brought back a feast of good things for the sufferer.

The picquet had been seduced by her eloquence to send her to Headquarters, under charge of a guard which watched her carefully as a probable spy. The General in command had seen fit to allow her to carry away such trifling articles as the Commission people would be willing to give, and although the chances were even that the gifts would be used in building up some wounded rebel, still the earnestness and the apparent truthfulness of her entreaty for relief overbore all scruples; the old fashioned vehicle was loaded with the wished for supplies, and the suspicious guard escorted the cargo beyond the lines.

The trip was thereafter repeated week by week, and when letters were at length received in answer to those deposited by the fair messenger, postmarked among the Green Mountains, her triumph was complete, and her draft good for anything the Sanitary treasury contained. The only lingering doubt was in regard to the enormous amount of whiskey the invalid required. Mrs. Van Metre, however, explained that it was needed for diplomatic as well as medicinal purposes. Of course it had been bruited about among the neighbors that the miller's wife was nursing a Federal officer. In that region now abandoned to the rule of Mosby and his men, concealment was essential. Therefore the old men who had heard of the convalescent must be taken into confidence and pledged to secrecy, a course rendered possible only by the liberal use of the *Spiritus Frumenti.* Under the influence of such liquor as had not been guzzled in the Valley since the peaceful days of Buchanan, the venerable rascals were easily convinced that such a shattered life as that of the Lieutenant could not greatly injure their beloved Confederacy.

Five weeks after Bedell received his wounds, our army was encamped on Cedar Creek, and Sheridan was in Washington. The Lieutenant greatly needed his valise from our baggage wagons. Therefore a journey of twenty miles up the Valley was planned, which brought our heroine and her little neice to the army again, with a few words traced by the maimed right hand of her charge as her credentials. Our feelings of wonder and admiration were most intense, as we learned from her simple story, that our favorite who was dead was alive again, and felt how much true heroism her modest words concealed. She had plainly totally abandoned herself for weeks to the care of a suffering enemy, and yet she did not seem to realize that she deserved any credit for so doing, or that every woman would not have done as much. We loaded her with the rude attentions of the camp, and she spent the night comfortably (from a military point of view) in a vacant tent at General Getty's headquarters. The desired valise was then at Winchester, but she obtained it on her return.

The next daybreak found us fighting the Battle of Cedar Creek. Amid the mounting in hot haste and the thronging confusion of the morning's surprise, General Getty found time to commit his terrified guests to the care of an orderly, who by a circuitous route conducted them safely out of the battle.

While our army was near Berryville in September, some of General Getty's staff-officers had called upon Mrs. Van Metre, and had persuaded her to prepare for them a meal or two from the army rations, there being a magnetism in female cookery that the blades of the staff were always craving. In her visit to the army just mentioned, she learned that one of those casual acquaintances had fallen at the former battle of the Opequan, and that his body was still lying somewhere on that wide battle-field. Seizing the earliest opportunity, after her return, she personally searched all through the territory between Opequan Creek and Winchester, amid the carrion and the graves, until she found at last the rude board with its almost obliterated inscription that fixed the identity of the too scantily covered corpse. Shocked at the sight, for the rain had exposed the limbs, and the crows had mangled them, she procured a coffin and laborers from Winchester, and had the remains decently interred in the cemetery there at her own expense. Then she addressed a letter to his friends giving them the information which she possessed, and they subsequently recovered the relics, thanking God and their unknown benefactor.

We heard nothing further from the Lieutenant for months. We eventually learned, however, that after a long period of such careful nursing, varied only by the weekly errand of Mrs. Van Metre to Harper's Ferry for letters and supplies, the prudent Doctor at last gave his consent that Bedell should attempt the journey home. Armed now with a pair of Sanitary crutches, he doubted not that he could make his way, if he once could reach the Union lines. But the difficulty of getting to Harper's Ferry cost him much anxiety. Though at various times forty guerillas together had been in and about the house where he lay, the watchful care of his protector had thus far kept them in ignorance of his presence. This journey, however, was likely to prove even more difficult to manage. At length one of the toddy-drinking neighbors, while relating his trials and losses, chanced to mention the seizure by our troops, of a pair of his mules months before, and the fact that a negro had since seen them in the Martinsburgh corral. A happy thought struck the Lieutenant; he at once assured the old gentleman that if he could only be placed (what there was left of him) in safety at the Ferry, the mules should be returned. The promise might perhaps be considered rash, seeing that Martinsburgh was twenty-five miles from Harper's Ferry, under a different commander, that it was very decidedly unusual to restore property seized from the enemy for government use, that the chattels were probably long ago far up the Valley, and especially that Bedell could not have, in any event, the faintest shadow of authority in the premises. But the old man jumped at the offer and the bargain was struck.

It was decided that Mrs. VanMetre should accompany the Lieutenant home, both for his sake as he was yet months from recovery, and for her own, as she had now lived for years in unwonted destitution and anxiety, while a quiet, comfortable home was thenceforth assured to her by her grateful charge until the return of peace; and who knew if she might not in some way regain her own husband, as she had restored another's!

So the party was made up and the journey commenced. The officer was carefully hidden in a capacious farm-wagon, under an immense heap of straw, and though two marauding parties were met during the day, the cheerful smile of the well-known jolly farmer disarmed suspicion. The escape was successful. The clumsy vehicle drew up before head-quarters at

Harper's Ferry, and Bedell, saluted once more by a sentinel as he doffed his hat to the flag he had suffered for, headed the procession to the General's room.

The unique party told its own story. The tall Lieutenant, emaciated, staggering on his unaccustomed crutches, the shrinking woman, timid in the presence of authority though so heroic in the presence of death, and the old Virginian aghast at finding himself actually in the lion's den, but with the burden of an anxious longing written on his wrinkled face,—each character so speaking, the group needed only this simple introduction: "General, this man has brought me in, and wants his mules!"

General Stevenson, warm-hearted and sympathetic, comprehended the situation at once. He made the party seat themselves before him and tell him all their story. He fed them at his table and lodged them in his quarters. He telegraphed for a special leave of absence for the officer, and secured free transportation for both him and his friend, and finally, most surprising of all possible good-fortune, he sent the venerable charioteer to Martinsburg, the happy bearer of a message that secured the restoration of his long-eared quadrupeds.

On the next day the Lieutenant and Mrs. VanMetre went on by rail to Washington, where of course every one treated them kindly, and gave them all possible assistance. When the paymaster had been visited and all preparation made for their journey north, it was determined to make an effort to secure the release of the rebel prisoner. So it came about that the quasi-widow and the crippled officer called together upon Secretary Stanton. The busiest of all busy men found time to hear their story, and despite the "stony heart" attributed to him by his enemies, he was deeply affected by the touching tale, and the ocular demonstration of its truth in the person of the wounded soldier. Tears rolled down his cheeks as he gave the order requested, earned by acts that few women would have dared; and the couple with glad hearts, crossing the street to the office of the Commissary General of Prisoners, presented the document to the clerk in charge to be viséd. But here another difficulty arose. Some one had blundered, and on searching the records of the office the requirèd name could not be found. The cruel report was made that no such prisoner had been taken.

Nevertheless, Mrs. VanMetre's information had been direct and her conviction of some mistake was sure. They laid the case before General Hitchcock, then in charge of that office, and again the story was argument enough. With trembling hands the old gentleman endorsed the order: "The commanding officer at Fort Delaware will release any person the bearer may claim as her husband!"

The prison barracks were quickly reached. The commandant caused the thousands of grizzly captives to be paraded. File after file was anxiously, oh how anxiously! scanned by the trembling woman, and when the circuit was almost completed, when her sinking heart was almost persuaded that death instead of capture had indeed been the fate of the one she loved, she recognized his face despite his unkempt hair and his tattered garments, and fell upon the neck of her husband as he stood in the weary ranks.

A few days more and the two united families were at rest in Bedell's New England home.

IX.

OPEQUAN.

On September 16th the Fifth Vermont was broken up, the larger portion of the original members being mustered out; a small veteran organization remained, commanded by Captain Addison Brown of the Fourth, assisted by Lieutenants detailed from other regiments of the Brigade.

The time of service of the Fourth expired September 19th. The regiment went through the Battle of the Opequan on that day, and some of its losses were among the men who should have been at the time *en route* for Vermont. Colonel, afterwards Brevet Brigadier Gen. George P. Foster remained in command of the portion of the regiment left in the field, which retained its name, as in the case of the other regiments of the Brigade, without the consolidation resorted to in troops from other States under similar circumstances.

Although we had at last successfully quieted the demonstrations of the enemy, which had excited so great apprehensions at times during the last three months, it had also become apparent that the rebels would not leave the Valley nor abandon their still threatening attitude toward Maryland and Pennsylvania until they were driven away. Lieutenant General Grant therefore paid our army a visit for the purpose of ascertaining the precise situation of affairs, and deciding on the question of an active campaign. He found Sheridan eager for a battle, and in his official report says: "he" (Sheridan) "explained so clearly the location and condition of the two armies, and pointed out so distinctly the method he should pursue if left at liberty, that I saw no instructions were necessary except the simple words, Go in!" He further says that he asked if the movement could not be commenced on the following Tuesday, the visit being on Saturday. Sheridan answered that he would be ready to move on Monday at day-break.

Grant returned Saturday evening. On Sunday a supply train arrived, five days' rations were distributed, the same wagons removed the sick and the superfluous baggage, and at night we knew that we were ready for some serious movement which the uncertain morrow was sure to bring.

Gen. L. A. Grant, having obtained a few days leave of absence, and not crediting the rumors of an advance, went to Harper's Ferry with the train, where he spent the next day listening to the sound of the cannon, and anxiously expecting news from the battle-field. His absence left Colonel Warner of the 11th in command of the Vermont Brigade; a West Point graduate, but with little previous field experience, he developed abilities on this occasion that for the remainder of the war gave him a Brigade of his own, and deprived his regiment of his valuable services.

It will be remembered that the Opequan Creek was between the two armies, four or five miles to the west of us, but diligently guarded by Early. A portion of his

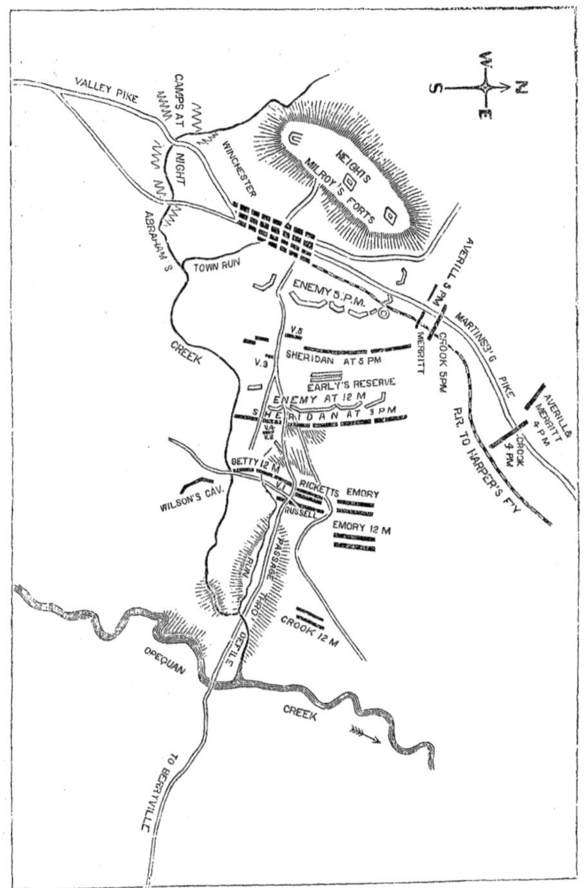

PLAN OF THE BATTLE OF

THE OPEQUAN.

19th September, 1864.

The successive positions of the Vermont Brigade are indicated as follows :—V. 1, V, 2, etc.

army was near Bunker Hill, ten miles north of Winchester; the rest occupied the hills and plains, covering that city. Kershaw's division, it was said, had just disappeared up the Luray Valley—leaving us with a preponderance of about 4,000 men.

Our movement commenced at 3 o'clock Monday morning, September 19th, Getty's Division having the advance, the Vermont Brigade being the last in the Division. Striking directly across the country, at first in the darkness, we presently reached the main road from Berryville to Winchester, and moved down it to the crossing of the Opequan. This stream is considerably below the level of the adjoining country, and the road on its further side keeps the low level of the stream for a mile or more, winding through a long tortuous wooded ravine, our unobstructed passage whereof was for the time a mystery. It seems that Wilson's Division of cavalry had already cleared the way and was then holding desperately a position that it had gained with considerable loss, but which proved a most admirable one in which to deploy our line of battle.

As we filed out of the ravine which toward the last was lined with wounded cavalrymen, we found Sheridan, his headquarters fixed on a conspicuous elevation, personally superintending from the commencement the operations of the day. It was to be our first battle under his command, as well as his first independent battle; the troops were hitherto destitute of all enthusiasm for him; fortunately, however, no impression save a favorable one had as yet been received, it being universally conceded that he had so far handled his army handsomely. And it was with great satisfaction that we found him in this early twilight at the very front, and under the fire of the enemy, carefully attending to details which we had been accustomed to see more celebrated commanders entrust to their staff.

Our Division promptly relieved the cavalry and formed its line facing west, the Third Brigade which was in advance going to what was to be the extreme left of the infantry line, resting on Abraham Creek; the First Brigade following, took up its position on the right of the Third, and our own Brigade filled the remaining distance between the First and the road on which we had reached the battle-field. It had been intended to place us in two lines, but the unexpected extent of the ground we had to cover forbade that formation. We were just on the hither edge of a narrow fringe of wood that concealed us from the enemy; the Sixth Vermont was thrown forward as a skirmish line perhaps one hundred yards to the further side of the little forest, and at once engaged the enemy's skirmishers.

Near us in the road at our right was a rebel field work taken by Wilson in the night. The hill on which it was situated commanded the country in both directions, and it was already occupied by a battery engaged in feeling the enemy, which was answered vigorously, many of the rebel shell plunging over into the troops as they successively came up the road.

Our Division thus formed in single line was the only Division on the south or left of the road. The Third

Division, Ricketts', followed us and prolonged the line across and on the north of the road, placing its two Brigades in two lines. The First Division, Russell's, came next, and was drawn up behind the Third as a third line or reserve, also somewhat overlapping the right of our Brigade.

Then to our surprise no more troops appeared, and our corps was alone confronting the enemy. There were two or three anxious hours, but Early was engaged in hurrying up his detachment from Bunker Hill, which this delay gave him ample time to do, and made no assault. It was said that the Nineteenth Corps being ordered to follow the Sixth, had filed into the road behind our wagon train, instead of keeping closed up on our column. It is certain that with this loss of time, from whatever reason it occurred, we lost the opportunity of attacking the enemy in detail, and gave him time to prepare for our reception. It was noon before the Nineteenth Corps had reached its place and was formed in three or four lines on the right of the Sixth.

Our men during the forenoon had been resting, sitting or lying on the ground. When at last the disposition was completed and the signal gun was fired, they sprang to the ranks, and the line advanced. Particular instructions had been received to the effect that the road was to give the direction of attack, and that the guiding regiment was to be the left regiment of the Third Division, just across the road from our right.

In passing through the bit of trees in our front, which was filled with underbrush, our line was necessarily thrown somewhat into confusion. When we emerged from the wood and the ground over which we must make our attack was developed, the prospect was appalling. The hill gradually sloped away before us, for a quarter of a mile, to a long ravine, irregular in its course, but its windings extending either way as far as we could see. The ascent beyond it was in most places sharp, and the enemy held its crest in force, perfectly commanding with musketry and artillery the long slope down which we must pass, though the acclivity on the further side of the hollow was so steep as to actually present a cover from their fire—if it could once be reached.

When this fearful prospect opened the line involuntarily halted, and the men threw themselves on the ground as was their wont when under fire. Our own Brigade was properly waiting for the movement of the guiding regiment which lay across the road a little to our rear, and which could not be prevailed upon to stir. To add to the peril of the situation, the road, instead of continuing straight on, as seems to have been expected, here made a bend to the left so that our original orders could not be obeyed without an amount of obliqueing that would have resulted in demoralization; from this cause our own Brigade was soon afterwards thrown into temporary confusion, and the Third Division was presently so disorganized as to be unable to resist a counter-charge made against it by the enemy.

At length the commander of the Brigade at our right crossed to our side of the road and urged us to set his men the example. Col. Warner took the responsibility, brought the Brigade to its feet, corrected the alignment, and gave the command to advance, which was promptly obeyed. The Third Division followed and the line was again in motion. But our point of direction was lost, for we were in advance of our guides, and when it was seen that owing to a curve in the ravine before us the cover on its further side could be reached much sooner by obliqueing sharply to the left, we took that direction almost by common consent, and left the road-side.

Our whole Brigade, every man at the top of his speed, making for the coveted protection of the hill beyond us, plunged pell mell into the hollow. The troops at our right and left were lost sight of. The ravine was of some considerable width and its bottom was marshy, being the head waters of a little branch of Abraham Creek. The steep slope on its further side was covered with evergreens six or eight feet high. To our intense consternation, as we reached its swampy bottom, we saw at our right, at short pistol range, at least a full regiment of the enemy drawn up in line near the point where the road crosses the hollow, in anticipation of our taking precisely the course we did, and firing coolly, as rapidly as they could load, directly along our line, thus enfilading us completely. Its position is indicated on the plan. The slaughter was for a few moments murderous. We could not retreat, for we should again enter the fire that had been mowing us down in the charge, now cut off by the hill before us.

We therefore floundered on, our coherence entirely lost, entered the clusters of evergreens through which the cruel bullets whistled fearfully, and at last, a confused mass at best, those of us who escaped unhurt reached comparative safety under the very crest of the hill, and high above the deadly hollow.

We now opened fire for the first time during the day, in the direction of the regiment or brigade that had so frightfully thinned our ranks, but they were almost out of reach from us, as well as we from them. At this moment, however, the Third Division approached them and they filed away.

When this was discovered, and after gaining breath, our own advance was resumed, but with little pretence at order. Emerging upon the plain before us at the summit of the hill we had climbed, we again turned obliquely towards the road and charged upon a long breastwork filled with rebels, in our immediate front. The retreat of their comrades from the ravine apparently demoralized them; many fled, many more were captured; in fact as we clambered over the parapet it seemed as if the prisoners who then surrendered exceeded in number our entire Brigade.

But we did not stop to count them or to care for them. The principal position of the enemy in this portion of the field had now been gained, and we rushed onward toward the distant spires of Winchester, with shouts and cheers, now thoroughly excited by our unexpected success. A battery of the enemy was before us but it limbered up and retired as we advanced. Several times it turned, fired a round of canister, and resumed its flight. At our left the other Brigades of our Division were seen moving on in our support. At our right an unfortunate ridge now rose, parallel with our line of advance, along the top of which ran the road so often referred to, and which hid our friends from view; we could only hope that they were equally successful, and push wildly forward. A point was reached probably three-fourths of a mile beyond the entrenchments where we had captured the prisoners, when luckily a ditch running across our path suggested cover and a pause. This ditch was reached only by the colors of the Fifth, with perhaps two hundred men from the various regiments. Exhausted with running they opened fire as vigorously as they could, but a line of rebels was seen gradually collecting in their front, as the fugitives were rallied, and the position held by our troops was presently dangerously threatened. And now to their dismay, the Brigade on the higher ground to their left saw reason for retiring and called to them to follow. What it could mean they did not know, but it seemed prudent to withdraw, if only for the purpose of keeping up the connection. An officer sent to investigate soon reported that at least a Division of the enemy were far behind their right in an orchard which they supposed had been carried by the Third Division. Orders were given therefore to fall back to the line of the army following the low ground on the left, thus keeping under cover of the hill at the right, the enemy meantime being absorbed in their movement against Ricketts; and thus the detachment successfully escaped from its dangerous position and re-formed with the balance of the Brigade near the works we had carried, being as before on the right of the other Brigades of our Division, connecting with and at first even in front of the support which was put in to meet the emergency.

We afterwards learned that a break had taken place on the right which for a time seemed likely to result in complete disaster. The report in our Corps was, that the Nineteenth, advancing through a long stretch of forest and at first successful, had afterwards been repulsed, and fled in disorder, many of the fugitives even going back to the Creek, and that our Third Division had been checked soon after we lost sight of it, presently becoming more or less involved in the flight of the Nineteenth Corps. On the other hand Gen. Emory, commanding the Nineteenth Corps, in a letter published in the *World*, which was fortified with affidavits, insisted that the break began at the right of our Third Division, which led to the turning of his left and the consequent retiring of his Corps. The official reports disagree as much as the letters of the correspondents, who of course reflected the opinions of the several headquarters to which they were attached, and who created considerable ill-feeling by the discrepancies in their accounts, and by their insinuations; the truth is probably between the claims of both, and the real cause of the enemy's temporary success seems to have been the unfortunate bend in the road above mentioned, which interfered with and destroyed the symmetry of our first advance. Our

Third Division obliqued to the left as it moved against the enemy, following the order to guide on the road, (there were few or no fences in that vicinity) and so left an interval between its right and the Nineteenth Corps, which appears to have gone in impetuously and with little order; the enemy presently made a counter-charge, and, luckily for them, struck the gap with a heavy force, crumbling off the troops on either side of it, and causing the troops on each side of the interval to think that the others had let the enemy through. The front line of the Nineteenth Corps was almost entirely disorganized, and was replaced by the second line, while only the right of our Third Division was broken up, its left with our own Division merely retiring a short distance under orders, as was necessary in order to keep a continuous front.

At the critical moment General Wright, who was for the day in command of the Sixth and Nineteenth Corps, though (as he says) "it was too early in the battle to choose to put in the reserves, still, seeing that the fate of the day depended on the employment of this force," promptly ordered in the First Division with two batteries; it marched gallantly down, with its full Division front, to the very face of the enemy, relieving the Third Division, which, re-forming, presently took up its position still further to the right, where the interval had before been left. Sheridan held back General Upton's Brigade of the First Division until it could strike the flank of the charging column of the rebels, when it made the most remarkable and successful charge of the day;

completely breaking up the rebel assault, and permitting our shattered line again to knit itself into coherence. General Upton was there wounded and the brave unostentatious Russell, the idol of the Division he commanded, was shot dead, while personally employed restoring the broken line.

The two hours following were spent in re-arranging the troops, issuing ammunition, and making dispositions for another advance. The Sixth Vermont, skirmishers through the morning, had properly allowed us to pass them in our first charge, but subsequently moving forward, accidentally joined the Third Division, where they gained great credit during the remainder of the day. The whole position now held by the Sixth Corps was that occupied by the enemy at noon. Getty's Division had been entirely successful, and had completely wiped out everything that had confronted it; the Vermont Brigade in particular met as determined resistance as any portion of the line could have done, besides passing through the terrible enfilading fire in the ravine, and not only drove back the enemy and held its ground firmly without assistance, but actually captured hundreds of prisoners, fairly finishing the battle in its front; the rest of the army not being equally fortunate, we afterwards had it all to fight over again.

Captain, afterwards Major Templeton, an exceedingly gallant officer of the Eleventh Vermont, had during the previous campaign excited considerable amusement in the Brigade by constantly carrying in his hands on the march a camp-chair, from the comfortable elevation whereof he was wont at the halts to smile serenely, in his rather boisterous way, at the ungainly rest obtained by other officers who were forced to sprawl themselves out upon the ground for rest. The exigencies of his retreat from the ditch mentioned above proved too great for the Captain's equanimity and he reluctantly abandoned his cherished chair to the tender mercies of the foe. When we formed, his loss was at once seen and he was ridiculed unmercifully, but he successfully redeemed himself by recapturing his furniture in the subsequent advance.

The Rebel line was now contracted, taking up a new position nearly two miles from that which they first attempted to hold, and occupying some old works surrounding the northern and eastern sides of the city of Winchester. Regular skirmish lines were thrown out on both sides and the artillery planted in advantageous positions.

Meanwhile General Sheridan was making his dispositions for a combination which proved decisive. General Crook's command had crossed the Opequan further to the north, and had been kept in reserve behind the Nineteenth Corps. As soon as our lines were firmly settled in the position secured by our first attack, Crook was put in motion to encircle and double back the rebel left. He was assisted by Averill's and Merritt's cavalry, and was entirely successful. Their detour was somewhat long and the day was fast waning, but the movement was hurried to the utmost, being supervised by Sheridan himself who found it utterly impossible to conduct a battle from a "commanding eminence" in the rear, as he at first attempted to do. As soon as he saw that the plan was in process of successful execution, he personally inspected the rest of his army and the enemy's position, riding at a terrible speed along the whole of our extended *skirmish line*, wheeling out from the storm of bullets only as he reached our own Division at the left of all, and pausing as he passed between the Brigades to exclaim, with eloquent profanity, "Crook and Averill are on their left and rear—we've got 'em bagged, by ——!"

The order to advance was soon received, and the line moved forward; not with the promiscuous disorderly rush of the former charge, but steadily and deliberately, aligning carefully by Brigades and by Divisions, we swept forward into the battle. The Vermont Brigade was fearfully enfiladed by a battery on our left, but every man kept his place in the ranks, and promptly obeyed Col. Warner's frequent orders. The Brigade headquarters flag was flying in the very battle line. The Second Division was still on the left, then the First and Third, the Nineteenth Corps still further to the right, and Crook's command on its flanking tour in the distance.

The line reached easy musket range of the enemy and opened fire. The artillery rattled up behind us and joined in the tumult. The batteries were nearer the front that day than we had ever before seen them, and General Sheridan's wish, expressed in the morning to Col. Tompkins, our Corps Chief of Artillery, that he might "see some dead horses before night" was amply gratified. At the time of the repulse of the first attack, Stevens' battery was ordered back by a staff officer who feared its capture, but Col. Tompkins held it to its work, pistol in hand, though the rebels were but two hundred yards from the muzzles of the guns.

On this second advance it again fell to the lot of the Vermont Brigade to be thrown forward beyond the rest of the line of battle of which it formed a part. We entered a corn field with stalks full ten feet high, and could do nothing of use until we reached its further limit, where it was bounded by a tomato garden, at the further side of which was a strong paling fence. Behind this fence we had halted when we opened fire. The enemy was in plain sight but a short distance before us and the men worked at their guns with the diligence of desperation. We were still enfiladed by the battery at our left, and we saw the Brigade on our right withdraw a short distance for better shelter behind the crest of a little hill. It seemed to us less dangerous to remain, and we clung to our position though losing rapidly. Major Buxton of the Eleventh was here shot dead, a bullet passing through his brain. Two or three years afterwards some lunatic created a sensation in Vermont by assuming the gallant major's name and title. The attempt gave a terrible shock to those who had seen the Major's remains, for his death was so sudden that he did not stir from the position in which he was lying with his face to the ground among his men.

Presently the line of the enemy before us was seen

to waver and melt away: many had fallen, others could not endure the deadly fire, and at last we caught a vision that redeemed Sheridan's assertion. The whole left of the enemy rushed past us toward our left in the wildest disorder. Crook and Averill had done their duty. Merritt, Custer and Lowell were madly urging the pursuit. They caught up with the mass of fugitives directly in front of our position, taking flags and cannon and thousands of prisoners.

The Brigade rose as one man, rushed at the fence that had partially protected us, and as it fell, passed over it into the open plain. The whole army was seized with the same impulse and strode joyfully forward, a huge crescent, with waving flags and wild hurrahs. The scene was wonderful. The infantry kept a rapid march and the alignment seemed complete. "Beautiful as an army with banners," is a figure full of meaning and its power was then completely realized. And in that joyful mood, conscious of strength and of victory, we closed upon the city as the evening fell. An attempt was made by the enemy to rally in some forts which were built by General Milroy in 1862, on a hill west of the city, but it was soon abandoned, and they fled in confusion up the Valley pike.

Our brigade was halted at the edge of the town near a vineyard covering perhaps an acre of ground, filled with grapes, ripe and abundant. The day's work had allowed no time to eat or drink and the opportunity thus offered was improved to the fullest extent. While we were thus regaling ourselves with the luscious fruit General Sheridan came by, and was saluted with the wildest cheers. Since the time of McClellan it had been a point of pride with the Brigade not to cheer its officers; but on this occasion tumultous hurrahs came unbidden from the bottom of every heart and conventional restraint was forgotten.

The Battle of the Opequan was the first occasion in which the new administration of affairs presided over by Lieutenant General Grant completely satisfied and compelled the approval of the many soldiers of the Vermont Brigade who were thoroughly wedded to the love of the old *régime.*

Meanwhile the cavalry had dashed furiously through the city, and on towards Newtown, but it was presently recalled, and the army bivouacked for the night on the South side of Winchester near Abraham's Creek. A night pursuit was physically impossible after such a day, but on the morrow we followed the enemy twenty-five miles to their fortress at Fisher's Hill.

The battle of the Opequan was an entire and complete success. It was fought between two armies nearly equal in size, and in a country for the most part free from trees —a "fair field fight." The enemy were at first surprised by Wilson, but concentrated in time to repulse the first general attack, losing however their best position. Then they were outflanked and almost surrounded on an open plain, hardly escaping with the loss of 4,400 prisoners, five cannon, many flags, nine generals (six wounded and three killed), 5.000 men killed or wounded, and much material captured. Their wounded were left in our hands, and the Rebels never revisited the lower Shenandoah Valley.

Gen. Wright in his official report spoke of the battle in the following terms:

The battle of the Opequan affords a rare example among the many hard fought fields of this war in which all the arms of the service co-operated with full effect. Infantry, Cavalry and Artillery had their full share in the operations of the day, and their movements were in entire harmony. The artillery of this Corps alone expended eighteen wagon loads of ammunition and all with good effect upon the results of the conflict. All my batteries were effectively engaged.

Sheridan telegraphed General Grant at 7.30 P. M., as follows:

I have the honor to report that I attacked the forces of Gen. Early on the Berryville pike at the crossing of the Opequan, and after a most stubborn and sanguinary engagement which lasted from early in the morning until 5 o'clock in the evening, completely defeated him driving him through Winchester. * * * * * * The conduct of officers and men was most superb. They charged and carried every position taken up by the rebels from Opequan Creek to Winchester. The rebels were strong in numbers and very obstinate in their fighting. I desire to mention to the Lieutenant General commanding the army, the gallant conduct of Generals Wright, Crook, Emery and Torbert and the officers and men under their command. To them the country is indebted for this handsome victory.

PHILIP H. SHERIDAN,
Maj.-Gen. Commanding.

At 1 the next morning he also sent the following dispatch to General Stevenson at Harper's Ferry: "We fought Early from daylight till between 6 and 7 o'clock. We drove him from Opequan Creek through Winchester, and beyond the town. * * *

We have just sent them whirling through Winchester, and we are after them to-morrow. This army behaved splendidly.

P. H. SHERIDAN.

The next morning the New York *Tribune* expressed the relief which this victory had brought to the loyal heart of the nation, in an editorial, commencing with the following stirring words:

"Hurrah for Phil. Sheridan! And for his gallant army! And for the Union which they fought for on Monday! And THANK GOD for the great victory which they won!

"We care not to repress the grateful exultation which we can but feel over this splendid success. It went with a thrill to the heart of every loyal man who heard it yesterday morning, and with a chill to the heart of every traitor in Richmond and in New York. Consciously or unconsciously it struck every one as the turning point of the great Virginia campaign, and it flashes upon us as the First Victory in the Valley of the Shenandoah which hitherto has been to us a Valley of Humiliation and almost of Despair. We remember no Victory in this War which has more suddenly and joyfully awakened the sympathies of the North; nor one which has been welcomed with a more enthusiastic delight."

The casualties of the Vermont Brigade were as follows:

REGIMENTS.	KILLED.	WOUNDED.	MISSING.	TOTAL.
2d	3	29	0	32
3d	0	26	4	30
4th	1	15	0	16
5th	6	22	0	28
6th	5	46	0	51
11th	8	85	6	99
Total,	23	223	10	256.

Major Charles Buxton and Captain Dennis Duhigg of the 11th were killed. Sumner H. Lincoln, Adjutant, afterwards Colonel, of the Sixth was wounded early in the day; Capt. James E. Eldridge of the Eleventh was also wounded severely, and Capt. Darius J. Safford slightly.

On the next day Col. Warner was assigned to the command of the First Brigade of our Division which he held with credit to the close of the War, becoming a Brigadier General presently; its commander, Gen. Wheaton, succeeded the lamented Russell in the command of the First Division. Gen. Grant being still absent, Col. Foster of the Fourth Vermont now commanded our Brigade. The Eleventh was thenceforward under Lieutenant Colonel (afterwards Colonel) Charles Hunsdon, its Battalions being commanded by Majors Walker and Sowles.

X.

FISHER'S HILL.

THE battle of the Opequan just described, and the wonderful day at Cedar Creek on the 19th of October, hereafter to be described, are much the best known of Sheridan's Valley battles. But among his soldiers the idea was current, and still prevails, that the battle of Fisher's Hill, with its unusual amount of careful reconnoitring and skillful manœuvring, resulting in almost incredible success, displayed even more military genius than either of the first named fields. The men who for two days faced those bristling fortresses, wondering if the dislodgment of their garrison could be possible, can never sufficiently applaud the skill that won them. The surprise of the enemy was here complete, though accomplished in broad daylight, and requiring the expenditure of much time and great strength in traversing the long and laborious distances required. The plan was matured a day and a half before its execution, and its success depended almost as much upon a correct estimate of the *morale* of the hostile armies, as upon the strategic skill displayed in perfecting the intricate dispositions involved in the plan of assault, and executing the scheme just as it was originally conceived. The reason why this battle has faded almost entirely from the memory of the average reader, and has even been almost entirely overlooked by our historians, is simply its wonderful and most extraordinary result. It was gained with so little loss that the overwhelming nature of the defeat inflicted is forgotten.

On the morning after the battle of the Opequan our whole army was in vigorous pursuit of the enemy before daybreak. Evening found us halted in his presence.

Thirty miles south of Winchester, the noble Valley being now narrowed from twenty miles to five, and the River still clinging to the mountains on its eastern side, a line of hills stretches across the country from the Shenandoah to the Blue Ridge (which is here called the Little North Mountains); broken hills, now receding and anon advancing as they follow the windings of a little stream, or mountain brook, called Tumbling Run, on their hither side, which wanders from the last named mountains easterly into the Shenandoah, hills high and commanding, crowned with earthworks and artillery, separated by rugged ravines which were blocked up with slashed and fallen timber, every rod of hill and hollow well guarded by rifle pits and abattis and bayonets. These hills and the stream run at right angles to the pike by which we were marching up the Valley to the South, and they are confronted on this side of the brook in part by wooded elevations and in part by level meadows. Beyond them in the centre of the Valley rises Round Top, a curious lofty height, almost a mountain, entirely covered with forest, save where a wide path had been cleared directly over its summit to fit it for a signal station, in which capacity it commanded most admirably every regiment of Early's army at its immediate foot, and equally admirably every company of Sheridan's force and every mile of turnpike as far as Winchester, except as woods scattered here and there might mask the ground.

Along the hills beneath this natural watch-tower the Rebels had drawn up their lines. In order to reach them Tumbling Run must be crossed, and the heights of Fisher's Hill must be wearily climbed in the face of their muskets and artillery. On their right was the Shenandoah, on their left the Little North Mountains, carefully picqueted as far as the enemy supposed a goat could climb. The position had been selected years before by Stonewall Jackson as the strongest in the Valley, and was by him entrenched and used as a constant rallying place, or sallying place, as the occasion might suggest. A half written letter found in the works after we had carried them, spoke of the Rebel army as secure in a "haven of rest."

Fisher's Hill was thus always ready for rebel occupation, and had been confronted once before by Sheridan, who then deemed it prudent to withdraw. Now, however, he was at liberty to strike the enemy according to his best discretion, and had also yesterday inflicted upon them a terrible blow. His army was eager in pursuit; the rebels were disheartened in retreat; we were satisfied that our commander was energy personified, though we yet feared an order for some reckless assault, scarcely dreaming that it was possible even with the heaviest loss to carry the Hill; the enemy were still ready to fight with determination, as long as they were sure that they were not out-generaled, but were infected with a want of confidence in their leader sure to ruin them if they saw any cause to waver. All these considerations Sheridan appreciated and laid his plans accordingly.

On the evening of September 20th the Nineteenth Corps was placed in the front along the meadows whence the turnpike sprang across the massive sloping bridge of masonry, and up the steep ascent of the hills in the possession of the enemy, the village of Strasburg being their headquarters. An interchange of cannon shot proved that our day's march was ended, and our passage up the Valley was to be here disputed. The rest of the army filed into the woods north of the village, and bivouacked for the night. At break of day General Sheridan made a careful reconnoisance and commenced his dispositions.

The Sixth Corps was to extend the line to the right of the Nineteenth across the Valley, and Crook's command, or, as it was usually called, the Eighth Corps, was again, as at the Opequan, to perform the part of the hammer that breaketh the rock. The cavalry had been sent up the Luray Valley, in order, if possible, to reach the enemy's rear at Newmarket, and cut off his retreat in the event of our success at Fisher's Hill; one small Division under Averill alone remained, which was of no assistance on account of the impracticable nature of the ground. Our loss in killed and wounded at the Opequan had been probably a little greater than Early's, and the absence of our cavalry more than counterbalanced the prisoners we had taken there. Kershaw's Division of the enemy had retired into the Luray before the former battle, but any superiority which we may have had on this occasion, was far overmatched by the wonderful natural fortification occupied by the rebels, which was being strengthened each minute by the vigorous use of the shovel and the axe. It was evident that a direct assault must fail. Bravery alone could never gain us the upper Valley.

After hours of study the brilliant scheme was laid which gave us victory without its usual price. It is said that Wright alone of all Sheridan's lieutenants regarded the project fixed upon as feasible, but our commanding General was "sure he could make it," relying greatly on his confidence that Early's brave army, distrustful of its leader, was on the watch for just such a catastrophe as finally befel it.

At 10 A. M. on the 21st our movement began. The Sixth Corps, filing off to the west, took its position on the prolongation of the line already held by the Nineteenth Corps, on this side of the Run. These two Corps covered a front of three miles or so, seizing such position and protection as best they could, while continually annoyed by the hostile batteries, and the sharpshooters on the enemy's skirmish line. However, most of us were under cover, hidden in the forests, or lying behind some crest of hill, or crouching beneath the walls with which the country is there striped.

A railroad, bereft of its rails, and in a terrible state of dilapidation generally, ran from north to south through the centre of both armies, piercing the hills with deep hewn cuts. Its lofty bridge across the brook had been burned years before, and its road-bed was guarded by artillery. Its vicinity was held by the Vermont brigade during the afternoon, and the constant whizzing of the shell from side to side over and around us was much more enlivening than agreeable. The bearer of Colonel Foster's headquarters flag was here killed by a sharpshooter's bullet; the only man killed in the Brigade at Fisher's Hill.

About a mile to the right of the railroad rose Flint's Hill, the highest elevation to be found on our side of the Run. The enemy, aware of its value to us, had occupied it, and instead of leaving it when they abandoned the remainder of the hither side of the stream, they evinced an unexpected determination to remain in possession of it. Twice or thrice during that afternoon fierce volleys of musketry had been heard from that direction, the meaning of which was discussed but not understood, the prevailing impression being that the enemy were trying to drive in our skirmishers, or perhaps making a sortie against our flank.

Suddenly just at dusk our Brigade was called to attention and hurried off at a double quick by the right flank. As we advanced, the firing all at once became sharp and sharper, until it was evident that no picquet line engagement was in progress. Presently we were halted in a wood just behind the rattling musketry, and in an admirable defensive position. It was now quite dark. No other idea occurred to us than that the rebels were

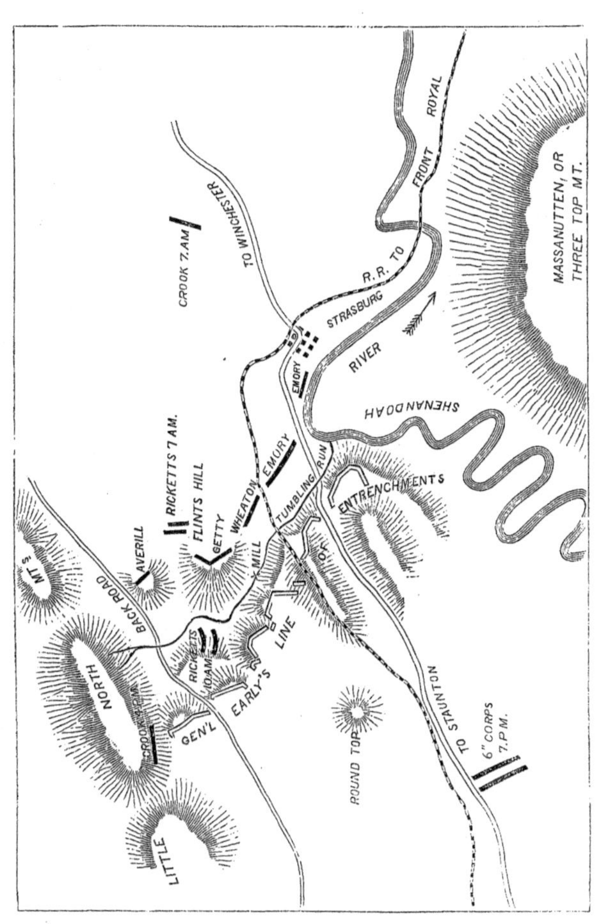

PLAN OF THE BATTLE OF

FISHER'S HILL.

22d September, 1864.

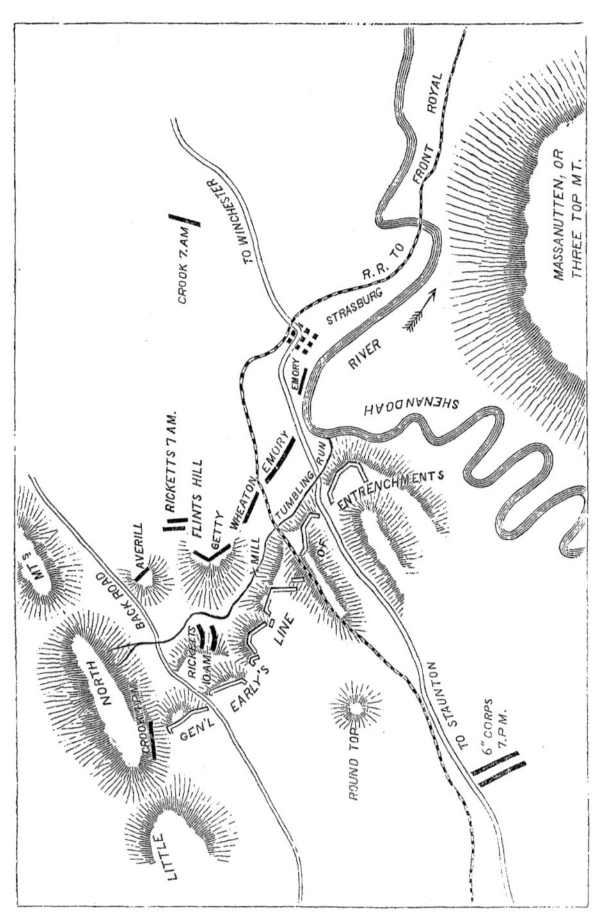

PLAN OF THE BATTLE OF

FISHER'S HILL.

22d September, 1864.

assaulting and driving in our skirmishers; and as the men threw themselves on the ground for rest after their race, and for cover, muskets were cocked and all preparations made to give any troops that might appear over the crest on which we lay a reception worthy of our reputation. But the tumult gradually ceased and a staff officer came in from the front, Lieutenant J. A. Lewis of the Eleventh Vermont. He was holding a handkerchief to his face to staunch the blood where part of his chin had been shot away by a bullet, but managed to say in explanation, "Warner has carried the hill!" It was well for Warner and his Brigade that they succeeded, for if they had failed and come back upon our rifles we should inevitably have fired upon them in the darkness. His Brigade had been assigned to the task which several times already had been unsuccessfully attempted; and by a dashing charge with fixed bayonets, under the eyes of all his commanders, he had won the position, driving a large body of the enemy across the brook to their main lines. Our Brigade had been hurried over to support him if necessary.

Thus the day's work ended with the accomplishment of its principal object; the coveted hill was gained, though Warner's Brigade lost more than the total casualties in the army on the morrow; the gallant Colonel was recommended for a Brevet in Sheridan's first dispatch, and received it promptly.

Our own Brigade soon felt its way up to Warner's right and into the open field. Entrenching tools were soon brought forward, and the night wore toilsomely away.

As the day broke on the 22d the scene was a surprising one. We had reached our then position through the woods, after night-fall, and now we were behind a solid entrenchment, traced boldly on the front of Flint's Hill, curving gracefully to the rear as the ground fell away on our right, and overlooking a beautiful field sloping down to the brook. The rebels were in plain view before us, scarcely half a mile distant across the stream, occupying a long entrenchment similar to our own, though with abattis in its front, which crowned a hill that brought them even above our level. After a half hour evidently spent in wondering at the mushroom growth that confronted them they fell to work diligently and laid down their shovels only to commence their flight.

It soon became apparent that the location of our Brigade was a fortunate one in enabling us to see and understand the operations of the day that had just dawned. Two rifled batteries promptly moved up and took their places in our line. Several others were halted just behind the top of the hill, where they were hidden from the view of the enemy; and presently Generals Sheridan, Wright, Crook, Emory, Averill, and others rode up with their staffs and orderlies. A telescope was planted upon its tripod in the field in front of our earthwork. General Crook after a hasty examination of the country to the distant right, rode rapidly away. The other officers continued to study the rebel line, waiting for the decisive moment. General Sheridan, especially, spent hours that day, sweeping with his glass to the right and the left, evidently bent on understanding precisely the task before him; occasionally pausing to remark to some by-stander, or to mutter to himself, "I'll get a twist on 'em, d—n 'em!"

During the forenoon General Ricketts moved his Third Division of the Sixth Corps in two lines from the woods behind our right, sweeping in grand display over the enemy's skirmishers, and finally halting at a very oblique angle to our line some distance in our front. The demonstration caused a great commotion among the rebels who evidently expected an immediate assault at that point where a receding sweep of their lines made a sharp angle; and they bent all their energies toward building a battery which should command this new imposing battle line. Their attention was thus entirely diverted from our position, and better yet, they were led to suppose that this Division was our extreme right flank, ("mistaking Ricketts' Division for our turning column," Sheridan says) and paid no attention to the vital point which Crook was aiming for. To add to their assurance of this view of our movements, Gen. Averill's cavalry ostentatiously picketed their horses on the very summit of a bare knoll on Ricketts' right and rear, as any soldier would infer, for the purpose of covering the outside of the army.

Meanwhile here and there through the trees behind us we could catch glimpses of the shining musket barrels of Crook's command, as they wound forth on their long and silent journey. Equipped only with rifles, cartridge boxes and canteens, keeping in the forests with the utmost care, avoiding every possibility of observation from the lofty natural watch-tower behind the rebel lines, these five thousand men crept from Strasburg to the distant mountain side. Our excitement momentarily increased as we came to understand the game, but our only relief was in watching the interchange of dangerous compliments between the skirmishers on either side of the brook below us. A large tree on the rebel side was particularly noticed as puff after puff of smoke was seen to rise from its branches, until Capt. Lamb, a grey-haired Rhode Islander who commanded half a dozen ten-pound Parrotts just at our left, deliberately and at the first attempt sent a screeching shell plump through its branches. A dozen 'Johnnies' dropped in great haste to the ground and scampered up the hill.

As the hours passed slowly by, Gen. Sheridan with more and more anxiety peered through his powerful telescope at the distant mountain side. Gen. Crook with his command of mountaineers had meanwhile reached the Blue Ridge and was clambering up its steep acclivities; no path, no guide—ordered simply to climb high enough to clear the enemy, then stealing south until they should overlap his flank, to dash down the mountain and strike him like a thunderbolt. The point aimed for by their tedious circuit was perhaps four miles from Flint's Hill; the enemy's left bending far to their rear, and making Crook's undertaking much more difficult.

It was almost four o'clock when he at last attained

the coveted position and formed his men for the assault. The attack began at once. Just as we saw his glittering line emerge from the forest, our Brigade leaped over our breastworks and swept off by the left flank into the woods; we went down near the bank of Tumbling Run, the rebel canister and grape meanwhile rattling through the trees about us, and waited for the result of the flanking movement. All our batteries that had been massed behind Flint's Hill galloped madly through the openings left for the purpose in our parapet, wheeled into position in the beautiful field, and answered the distant cheer that announced the commencement of the charge with the roar of thirty cannon. Crook swept on without a halt. The rebel signal officer afterwards said that his Corps seemed to burst from the clouds. The enemy supposed them to have come over the mountains. The paralyzing murmur that they were outflanked crept through the rebel lines. The men lost heart for battle and the bravery of the officers was of no avail. And now Crook had nearly reached the position so long confronted by Ricketts, who, without waiting to effect a junction, advanced his line against the steep ascent, rushed upon the fort that had been built in his face that day, and took it at the first attempt. Staff officers shouting the glorious news galloped wildly to the left along the line, sending brigade after brigade to join the charge, and thus the whole army gradually swung into place like machinery, swelling the grand advancing wave. The Vermont Brigade at the commencement of its advance met a shallow mill-pond that had not been noticed in the forest, in some way floundered through, rushed up the hill to the rebel works, then turned to the left, and in a confused delirious mass, hurried on as best it might after the scattered enemy. Guns were fired wildly into the air and re-loaded as the soldiers ran; captured cannon were wheeled about and discharged at the panic-stricken foe in mad salute for our victory; General Sheridan with long black streamers waving from his hat joined our own division, exclaiming, "Run boys, run! Don't wait to form! Don't let 'em stop!" and when some answered, "we can't run, we're tired out," his reply was perhaps unmilitary but certainly under the circumstances judicious, "If you can't run, then holler!" and thus the wild pursuit was continued until we reached the turnpike where it crosses the very summit of Fisher's Hill. The Eleventh Vermont almost alone of the troops engaged in the charge retained a respectable organization, and this was owing to a peculiar artillery flag it carried, easily distinguished among the others, of yellow silk with large crossed cannon. General Crook sent this regiment across a deep ravine to drive away a few of the enemy still remaining on the hill between the turnpike and the Shenandoah. After this had been accomplished it returned by a long detour to the road, perhaps a mile beyond where it had left it, and waited for other troops to come up; the first man that appeared was Col. Foster leading the balance of the Vermont Brigade in line of battle to the south.

The enemy had now vanished into the forests and it was dark. While the various brigades were disentangling themselves, and the men were seeking here and there their respective regimental colors, the Nineteenth Corps appeared, from whose front near the pike the enemy had fled demoralized, almost before they commenced their advance. The troops of the Sixth Corps were drawn aside into the field and made a hasty supper, while the Nineteenth Corps passed them in pursuit of the enemy with General Sheridan at its head. The Sixth Corps followed the Nineteenth closely, Gen. Wright being again for the time in command of both Corps, making twelve miles during the night; Crook's command was obliged to return to Strasburg for its knapsacks and did not overtake the army for several days.

During the night Sheridan found time to pencil the following dispatch:

"6 Miles From Woodstock,
11.20 P. M., Sept. 22.

LIEUTENANT GENERAL GRANT:

I have the honor to announce that I have achieved a signal victory over the army of General Early at Fisher's Hill to-day. I found the rebel army posted with his right resting on the north fork of the Shenandoah, and extending along the Strasburg Valley west toward the North Mountain, occupying a position which appeared almost impregnable. After a good deal of manœuvring during the day Gen. Crook's command was transferred to the extreme right of the line on North Mountain, and then furiously attacked the left of the enemy's line carrying everything before him. While Crook was driving the enemy in the greatest confusion and sweeping down behind their breastworks, the Sixth and Nineteenth Army Corps attacked the rebel works in front and the whole army appeared to be broken up. They fled in the utmost confusion. Sixteen pieces of artillery were captured, also a great many caissons, artillery horses, etc. I am to-night pushing on down (*sic*) the Valley. I cannot say how many prisoners I have captured, nor do I know either my own or the enemy's casualties. Only darkness has saved the whole of Early's army from total destruction. My attack could not be made till four o'clock in the evening which left but little daylight to operate in.

PHILIP H. SHERIDAN,
Major-General."

And again from Woodstock:

"Sept. 23d, 8 A. M.

* * * "I do not think there ever was an army so badly routed. * * * I pushed on regardless of everything. * *

P. H. SHERIDAN."

The results of this battle can be briefly told. The carrying the strongest position in Virginia with the loss of scarcely two hundred men; the utter rout of Early's army which made no stand in all the eighty miles through which it was promptly pursued; the capture of 1500 prisoners, all the enemy's camp equipage, many colors, (on an elegant staff here captured our Brigade flag was afterwards mounted), and twenty-one guns, being all the artillery he had save three pieces which were planted near the pike; and what was perhaps most important of all in view of the scene to occur a month hence at Cedar Creek, the conversion of the whole army to the belief that General Philip H. Sheridan is not only a brilliant cavalry rider, an impetuous fighter, and the impersonation of warlike energy, but that he is also a careful, deliberate, pains-taking soldier, thoroughly versed in tactics and strategy, whose fiery zeal is controlled by most unusual discretion, and whose masterly skill curbs a spirit of the hottest mettle. In short that he is, as General Grant has frequently declared, competent to command all the armies of the United States against any enemy.

To show that the importance of this victory is not exaggerated above, I again quote from Gen. Wright's report. "The annals of the war present perhaps no more glorious victory than this. The enemy's lines, chosen in an almost impregnable position and fortified with much care, had been most gallantly carried by assault, capturing most of his artillery, a large number of prisoners, and sending his army 'on the run,' in the most disorderly manner, and all this, from the impetuosity of the attack, with an absurdly small loss on our part."

No members of the Vermont Brigade were killed, excepting the color-bearer above mentioned, who fell on the day before the battle; and the number of wounded was so small that no report of them was made.

XI.

A MONTH OF CAMPAIGNING.

On the morning of September 23d, we halted at Woodstock, twelve miles south of Strasburg. Here, to our great surprise, we were overtaken at daybreak by a supply train which had followed close at our heels through the night pursuit; and it caught us just in time for no issue of rations had been made since the day before the Battle of the Opequan. It was welcomed as a new proof of Sheridan's foresight, and at noon with haversacks well-filled again, the shrunken sides whereof had been eyed with great suspicion at the conclusion of our last hasty supper-hour, we resumed our march up the Valley, Averill being now in advance with his little Cavalry Division.

He soon reported that he had found two divisions of infantry in his front near Mount Jackson. Sheridan, disbelieving his story, promptly relieved him from his command and sent him back to Martinsburg, replacing him by General Powell. Meanwhile the afternoon was nearly lost and we camped beyond Edinburg, this side of Averill's infantry simulacrum.

Early in the morning of the 24th we again advanced, (the commencement of my sentence reminds me of a somewhat profane use of a sacred couplet, then common in our army,

> "Early, my God without delay,
> We haste to seek thy face—")

and soon passed through Mount Jackson. Here were several barracks, built long before by General Shields, now used as hospitals, and full of wounded rebels; the only one of them which was empty was most maliciously set on fire by some stragglers from our column, and entirely destroyed.

A few miles beyond this village all of Early's force remaining coherent were deployed in a strong position in order to check us and enable their train to get away. A little way behind their line the road was to be seen winding down the mountain's side, by which Torbert had been ordered to cross over from the Luray Valley to the enemy's rear. He had not yet been heard from, and was anxiously watched for, but the combination failed.

Meanwhile the ground on which the rebels were drawn up was so strong and their line so extensive that we were compelled also to go into line of battle. The Nineteenth Corps being pushed around to their extreme left however, they incontinently withdrew, and we hastened after at our best gait. Now commenced a wonderful race. When we reached the elevation which they had abandoned, we found a high plateau, nearly level, the road running through its centre, the country on each side somewhat hilly, but still favorable for our use—and we also saw the retreating rebels in the distance driving their trains before them. It was a beautiful day, clear and cool; every one at once perceived the situation of affairs. The Sixth Corps took the left of the road,

Getty in advance, his Division in parallel columns by brigades, so that the division line could at any time be formed in three minutes, the Vermont Brigade nearest the pike. The Nineteenth Corps was on the right of the road, its front in line of battle, a much more difficult, though more imposing and methodical mode of marching. Skirmishers were crowding on in front of all, who kept up a constant fusilade with the enemy's rear guard; two batteries also were with the advance, now galloping along the road to some high point far in front of the skirmish line, and now unlimbering and opening a furious fire upon the fugitives. Thus we chased the enemy through Newmarket to Sparta, twenty-five miles that day, thirteen miles without a halt and with the rebels in our sight. The Nineteenth Corps across the pike was a mile or two behind us when we gave up the pursuit. The enemy were too anxious to escape and we saw them no more.

The next day, the 25th, we encamped at Harrisonburg, while the cavalry, which had now joined us, went on to Staunton. We passed a very pleasant week in this vicinity, although rations were rather scanty. Our supplies were brought up by a series of supply trains or caravans, from Martinsburg, furnishing three days' rations once in four days. For the rest every man took care of himself, and there was no suffering. Many of the regiments thenceforward were followed by cows as well as pack-mules.

On the 29th a march of seven miles was made, to Mount Crawford, the farthest point we reached. Detachments were sent out to the numerous mills in the vicinity and a large supply of flour obtained. Major Safford, a practical miller from Morristown, Vt., ground and brought into camp a full day's ration for the entire Division. On the next day we returned to Harrisonburg and resumed our old line at the east of the village. On the 2d of October, five hundred picked men from the Vermont Brigade, under an enthusiastic staff-officer, scoured the adjacent mountains all day long, hunting for stragglers and guerillas, but finding little save cattle and apple-brandy.

We were now for two or three weeks entirely cut off from news of the war elsewhere, and the camps were full of the most improbable stories. Intelligence of the capture of Richmond and Jeff Davis seemed as reasonable as the story of Grant's utter and overwhelming defeat, and we had our choice of the probabilities, for both of these stories were retailed with the utmost positiveness. Once in a great while we managed to obtain a Richmond paper, our only reliable channel of information. Perhaps we might have been furnished regularly with them, but for the fact that stage communications were for some reason interrupted.

On the 6th of October we commenced our return down the Valley. No enemy could be found by the most diligent search and the question of supplies was becoming a serious one. There was not enough transportation in the Department to feed us at that distance from our base, and moreover the guerillas were attacking every train. A Provisional Division, organized as train escort, had rather a hard time of it, marching night and day, besides fighting almost as continually.

After a long day's march, we at last halted for the night on meeting a supply train, which was again exceedingly *apropos*. Gen. Grant came up with this escort and resumed the command of our Brigade.

About noon on the 8th we reached Strasburg, whence, though the day was very cold, many of us improved the opportunity to resume our acquaintance with Fisher's Hill, under more favorable circumstances than on the former occasion. At this time the cavalry turned round at Tom's Brook to wipe out Rosser, the new Cavalry General from Richmond who was expected to deliver the Valley but didn't, losing instead everything he had with him that went on wheels.

The march from Harrisonburg was memorable on account of the sight of burning barns, mills, and stacks of hay and grain. Pillars of smoke surrounded us through all of the three days, and though no houses were destroyed, everything combustible that could aid the enemy during the coming winter was burned, and all cattle and sheep were driven away.

On the 10th the Sixth Corps moved round the Massanutten to the vicinity of Front Royal in the Luray Valley, a point that General Augur was trying to reach by re-constructing the railroad through Manassas Gap. The attempt was subsequently given up, however, and Sheridan's army was supplied by the Baltimore and Ohio Railroad throughout the winter.

On the 13th the Corps was ordered to move at daylight, the rations issued the previous day to last us to Alexandria. It was reported that transports were to take us thence to meet Sherman in North or South Carolina. We marched some fifteen miles to the ford of the Shenandoah near Ashby's Gap, where, just as the leading regiments were commencing to cross, and when Wright and Getty were already in the stream, scouts reached us bringing orders from General Sheridan, and we bivouacked without crossing. At our dinner hour that day we had halted near a somewhat dilapidated but unmistakable country school-house. It did not appear clearly what feeling of impropriety or inappropriateness it excited among the soldiers, but suddenly and by a common impulse of wrath the brigade seized upon it for culinary purposes. It may have been on account of the importunity of hunger, rather than any indignation against the symbol of primary education, as a small country store near by soon suffered the same fate, though in a different way, the material of one being used to cook the contents of the other.

The next day, by a long and rapid march, again through Newtown and Middletown, we rejoined Sheridan's army and took up the position which we held until the Battle of Cedar Creek. It was fortunate for him and the country that he took the responsibility of retaining us in his command. He was led to do so from the fact that the enemy, now again at Fisher's Hill, had made a threatening reconnoisance; but as no further demonstrations appeared, Sheridan improved the present season of quiet by making a personal inspection of his new route to Washington, leaving us temporarily under command of General Wright. As there was still some apprehension of an attack we were under arms at four A. M., daily—but the precaution seemed needless and the order was presently discontinued.

On the 16th of October, the Sixth Vermont was mustered out, thus completing the term of service of all the regiments of the original Vermont Brigade. As in the case of the other regiments, the Sixth still maintained its organization under Lieutenant Colonel Sumner H. Lincoln.

XII.

CEDAR CREEK.

The now historic stream which gave its name to the remarkable battle which is the subject of the present chapter, is a shallow, rapid river, perhaps thirty yards wide, flowing across the Upper Shenandoah Valley just where it debouches into the Lower Valley, which it will be remembered, from Cedar Creek to the Potomac unites the width of the Upper Valley and the Luray. The Shenandoah here sweeps round the base of the rocky and precipitous Massannutten mountain, hugging its foot and turning to the east with a sharp right angle, at the very apex of which it receives the waters of Cedar Creek, coming from a prolongation of the new direction of the larger river. The turnpike from Winchester to Staunton crosses the Creek about a mile above its junction with the Shenandoah. Middletown is two miles this side of the bridge; Strasburg two miles beyond it. Hills, perhaps three hundred feet high, rise irregularly on each side of the Creek. The army was facing south; Gen. Crook's command lay on the left of the turnpike, occupying several hills which overlooked the junction of the two streams, their picquets protecting the left flank of the army, though without watching sufficiently the fords of the rivers. The Nineteenth Corps was across the pike on Crook's right, on other hills along the hither side of the Creek; the Sixth Corps was next in line and the last of the infantry; Getty's Second Division, on the extreme right of all, being refused so that it faced westerly; the Cavalry Corps lay at our right and behind us; picquets from our Division were four miles from camp, guarding, in connection with the cavalry, the line of the Creek clear across the Valley.

General Wright being now in command of the army, Gen. Ricketts succeeded to the command of the Corps.

Our position was a good one, and as far as human foresight could reach, a safe one, though perhaps too much reliance was placed on the demoralization of the enemy. In flanking it General Early adopted Sheridan's tactics at Fisher's Hill, where the same Eighth Corps that was first attacked and routed here, by climbing the mountain side, had turned the line which Early assured his men could by no possibility be flanked; the successful attack of Early at Cedar Creek was as admirable as our own at Fisher's Hill, and even more audacious, as it involved the double fording of a rapid river to commence with, and the certainty of complete destruction in case of failure.

It has always been somewhat of a mystery where Early obtained the troops with which he fought this battle. The previous engagements had cost him fully twelve thousand men *hors du combat*, including prisoners, and as many more in stragglers. Kershaw's Division, however, which had retired through the Luray Valley, had been recalled, and Pegram's Division had joined him entire from Longstreet's Corps. The scattered remnants of other divisions had been collected

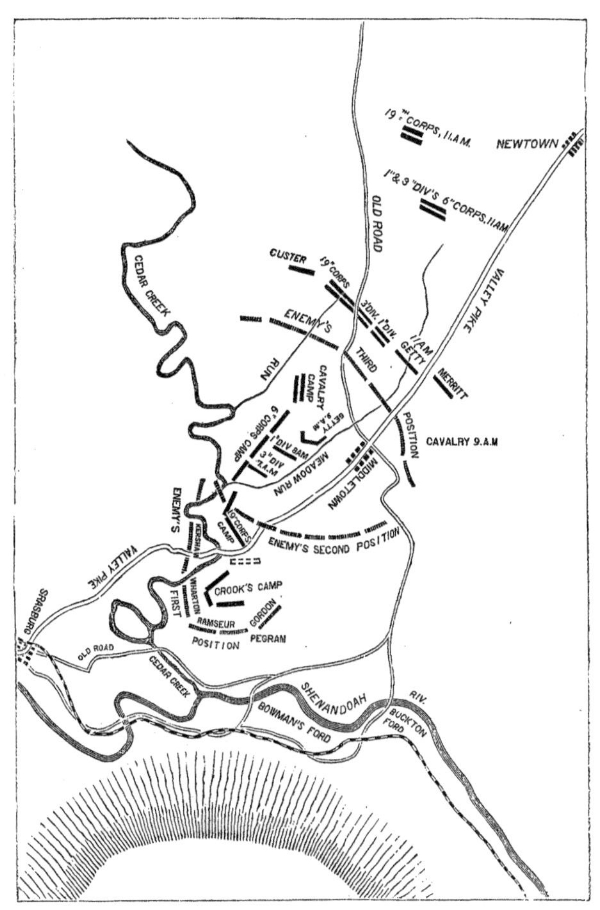

PLAN OF THE BATTLE OF

CEDAR CREEK.

19th October, 1864.

from their hiding places in the forests and the mountains. It is certain also that a large body, estimated by "Druid" at from twelve to fifteen thousand more, had been raised by the last relentless conscription in the vicinity of Gordonsville and Lynchburg. It has been asserted that many of these men were without muskets, hoping to gather arms on the field in our anticipated rout. Probably, however, but few unarmed men were in the enemy's lines. A letter from Richmond to a paper further south at the time in question says that the force thus concentrated was "good for" 50,000 men, and that 15,000 reserves were to be called out. This, however, was a greatly exaggerated estimate. Sheridan had received no reinforcements and we could not have had 25,000 men "present for duty equipped" including the cavalry which did nothing until evening. Early must have had 20,000 infantry at the very least. His plan was to attack us in detail and rout our Divisions successively, from the left; we shall see that he succeeded until he reached the last Division in the line, Getty's, which Sheridan truly says was the only Division of the Infantry which "confronted the enemy from the first attack in the morning until the battle was decided."

Every circumstance, save the difficulty of the ground, favored Early's project. The night was utterly dark; the morning chilly and raw, owing to a dense fog which did not lift until nine o'clock and which completely veiled all the movements of the enemy, whereas the position of our camps had been previously carefully studied and mapped by his officers from the summit of Three-top mountain. Between the base of the mountain and the Shenandoah river there was space amid the debris for a wagon road and a then dismantled railroad leading from Strasburg to Front Royal. The river was crossed near that village at dark on the 18th by the Divisions of Gordon, Pegram and Ramseur, which at once commenced cautiously picking their way down the rugged road and the railroad, no officer mounted, in the darkness and forest and fog, until they reached what is known as Bowman's Ford, outside of Crook's furthest picquets. Powell's Cavalry Division was still further down the river opposite Front Royal, and out of reach. Had the fords between Crook and Powell been carefully protected it is probable that the surprise could not have taken place. It had been supposed, and with great reason, that our right was the enemy's only feasible point of approach.

As the column reached Bowman's Ford, it again crossed the breast-high Shenandoah and stole in single file close up to the fires of our confident outposts, until at four A.M., the grey battalions had deployed, with Gordon on the right completely overlapping Crook's encampment.

That they were thus permitted deliberately to make ready for the charge seems almost incomprehensible. The videttes who should have given the alarm afterwards related that they heard a sound as of a going amid the rustling leaves through the night hours, but they were unable to comprehend its purport; it was even reported among the other portions of the army that Gen. Gordon actually relieved part of Crook's picquet line and then sent the men as prisoners to their rear.

The direction of attack was west; the enemy's right was drawn up facing the turnpike, reaching far towards Middletown, while his left followed the course of Crook's line, getting between his works and the Creek, and connecting with Wharton's Division which had meanwhile crossed the creek a little below the turnpike bridge. Early himself with Kershaw's large Division was near the bridge with artillery planted on the hills, ready to cross as soon as Crook should be swept aside, while his cavalry were on the back road far away to the west near the Little North Mountains.

It was at this latter point that the battle commenced; very early, probably before four o'clock, we were aroused by a dropping fire of musketry in that direction, at one time quite considerable in amount, but as it diminished soon we wrapped ourselves again in our blankets and resumed our sleep, fully confident that our picquets could take care of the reconnoisance or whatever it might be. The few prisoners reported lost from the Brigade in the day's battle, were taken at that time. Capt. C. J. Lewis of the Eleventh Vermont, an exceedingly careful officer, was in charge of our extreme right reserve post, and Col. Foster of the Fourth Vermont was field officer of the day. The cavalry on his right were deceived by the stale trick of an attack and a feigned retreat, leaving their posts to follow. A larger force instantly passed through the gap and fell with a yell upon the rear of the infantry reserves; the greater part of them escaped and after a rapid detour towards our camp, deployed into a rude skirmish line and still covered the Corps, keeping up a free fight on their own account until they knew from the sound of the battle behind them that our army had left its ground, when they came in and participated in the final charge of the day.

The alarm created by this little affair had almost subsided, when a sullen roar of musketry, dull at first but only too easily interpreted, arose from the distant left. It was the charge of the enemy in solid lines, without skirmishers, upon the works of General Crook. When the firing began, Early at once opened with his artillery from across the creek, thus raising a doubt as to the real point of attack. Crook's brigades could not even attempt to maintain their position or their integrity; the enemy captured the picquets who did not fire a shot, rushed upon the main line, which was first made aware of the attack by a full volley poured into their camp, and it was rapidly crowded towards the west. The men sprang from their tents and fled without boots or clothing save what they had worn through the night; the very tents were pulled off from some as they lay in their blankets; many with soldierly instinct placed themselves without orders behind the breastworks, only to find themselves flanked and taken in reverse file by file, each successively by the whole rebel column; and in simply time enough for the enemy in his impetuous charge to pass over the ground covered by the "Army of Western Virginia" that whole command was a disorganized, routed, demoralized, terrified mob of fugitives, their camp equipage left behind, officers and men all rushing to the rear in reckless dishabille. It was not afterwards seen as an organization during the entire day.

That these men were brave no one doubts; their previous brilliant conduct had amply shown it; but a night surprise, total and terrific, is too trying for the *morale* of the best troops in the world to survive.

The Nineteenth Corps across the pike had sprung to arms at the first sound of the conflict, the men for the most part leaving their tents and extra clothing as they stood, and forming their lines like soldiers. One Brigade under Colonel, since Brigadier General, and now Lieutenant Governor Stephen H. Thomas, of the Eighth Vermont, which regiment it included, was formed for the march at the time the fight commenced, having been ordered out on an early reconnoisance; it plunged at once across the pike into the woods, stemming the rout, and facing the enemy. Gen. Wright endeavored to use it as a nucleus on which to reform Crook's command, and so gain time to bring up the rest of the army to the strong line of the turnpike, but his hopes were disappointed; the Eighth Corps refused to rally, and in a few moments Thomas' Brigade was swept back overpowered, retiring sullenly and leaving in the forest the largest proportionate loss suffered by any brigade during the day.

The attacking column having now reached the pike, Early at once crossed the creek with Kershaw's Division and assumed command in person. He attacked the Nineteenth Corps without delay. That organization was as above mentioned drawn up in its works, some of the troops being actually formed on the reverse side of their entrenchments. But Gordon's powerful right extended far to Emory's rear; and the Nineteenth Corps, in turn flanked and enfiladed, although it offered an organized and energetic resistance, was soon crushed by piecemeal, and brigade after brigade, first losing heavily, fled in disorder.

General Wright and Sheridan's staff worked bravely and vigorously, endeavoring to stop the rout and reform the stragglers, the gallant General riding wounded over the field, his bleeding face bound with a handkerchief. But bravery simply could not arrest the torrent; the Sixth Corps was ordered in, but the excellent disposition of this Corps and the cavalry directed by Gen. Wright failed of success through lack of time, and on account of the fog.

Getty's Division, two miles to the right of Crook, heard all this firing with astonishment simply; we could only suppose that the attack was in front, for we did not dream that the position could be turned on the left, and we expected the easy repulse of the enemy; still we instantly struck tents, packed knapsacks, formed our lines, and were ready to move when called upon.

The Third Division, then the First, and lastly the Second, of the Sixth Corps being now moved by the left flank and by file left were successively put in the way of the charging column, each passing by the rear of the preceding Division and forming in *échelon* on its left, so that Getty's Division passed to the left of the corps, endeavoring to reach the high ground on the pike near Middletown. The cavalry from our right continued the same movement and passed behind us to our left and rear. But the right of the enemy's column kept along the creek toward our right flank after sweeping clear the entrenchments of the Nineteenth Corps, and our Third and First Divisions were successively attacked and overpowered by Early's now concentrated army. They were lost to our sight in the fog but we could hear the noise of their battle, and we knew that they were fighting desperately. Nearly every field officer in the First Division (Wheaton's) was killed or wounded. General Ricketts, in command of the Corps, was wounded almost mortally. The Tenth Vermont in the Third Division went back a long distance after commencing its retreat, in the face of the leaden rain, to recapture and save a battery from which the horses had been shot, dragging off its guns by hand. Twenty-four cannon had now been lost and the enemy had hardly been checked for a moment.

As Getty's Division moved by the left across the plain in the rear of the late camping ground, making as mentioned above, for the high ground near the pike, the prospect was dreary enough. I am utterly unable to describe the universal confusion and dismay that we encountered. Wagons and ambulances lumbering hither and thither in disorder; pack horses led by frightened bummers, or wandering at their own free will; crowds of officers and men, some shod and some barefoot, many of them coatless and hatless, few without their rifles, but all rushing wildly to the rear; oaths and blows alike powerless to halt them; a cavalry regiment stretched across the field, unable to stem the torrent; and added to the confusion and consternation the frequent sight of blood, ambulances, wagons, men, stained and dripping, with here and there a corpse; while the whistling bullets and the shrieking shell told that the enemy knew their advantage and their ground. It was a sight that might well have demoralized the Old Guard of the first Napoleon.

As our division reached Meadow Run (a branch of Cedar Creek) a deep brook that annoyed us continually during the operations of the day, we received a fire from the enemy's skirmishers in a piece of woods near by, which compelled General Getty to abandon his intention of reaching the pike and to go into line on the immediate left of the First Division, a little to its rear. The Fifth and Sixth Vermont, under command of Major Enoch E. Johnson of the Second then commanding the Fifth, and Major Walker's battalion of the Eleventh Vermont were ordered forward to clear the woods. Promptly deploying as skirmishers they advanced for the time successfully, reaching the further edge of the forest and halting under cover of the trees, so far to the front that they were much annoyed by the fire of our own batteries from behind the Division. The position was a good one, and a continuous line was arranged covering completely the whole Division front. Thus for the first time during the day the enemy was opposed by the regular formation of a skirmish line masking a line of battle. Still, the skirmishers in the confusion and the fog feared that there might yet remain some of our own troops in their front, and being almost literally in the dark, hesitated about opening fire. At last a scattered line was dimly seen approaching through the mist which felt no such hesitation, giving us a volley which at once convinced us that the skirmishers of the enemy were upon us. Their progress was stopped without difficulty, but a double line of infantry was soon made out moving forward in perfect array, the front line firing heavily as they came, evidently supposing that a large force was stationed in our little forest; and our skirmishers at once falling back, as was their duty, rejoined their Division, leaving several wounded where they fell.

Meanwhile Gen. Getty, forming his Division in two lines, had advanced across the Run to the prolongation of the line held by the First Division; but that command at last routed in turn by the heavy force of the enemy thrown against it, broke in confusion and fell back, passing through the artillery of the Corps. Getty was now left alone upon the field. Seeing a strong semi-circular crest behind the Run, he fell back about three hundred yards and occupied it with his Division, throwing Warner's First Brigade from the second line to the right of the Division in order to cover as much ground as possible, the Vermont (Second) Brigade being in the centre on Warner's left, and Bidwell's (Third) Brigade on Grant's left, Warner and Bidwell being partly covered by woods, but our own Brigade being in an open field.

Warner's Brigade was "in the air," all our troops in that direction having retired; Bidwell's left connected with a cavalry skirmish line, bending towards the rear. The position was on the whole an excellent one, however, notwithstanding there were no works, walls, or fences, the men lying down just behind the top of the hill, while a few skirmishers from each regiment were again sent forward over the ridge.

The assault was not long delayed. The enemy charged in full line of battle against our brigade, and the left of Warner's. They pressed their advance with great determination, but it was unavailing and they presently retired across the run into the fog, which from this time began to disappear. Our skirmishers again followed over the crest. The rebels now concentrated a terrible fire of artillery upon our position, and shell from thirty guns flew, screaming devilishly, over and among us. The men hugged the ground, being somewhat covered by the hill, and owing to the cover thus obtained, the loss, as General Getty says, "was lighter than could be expected."

After a cannonade lasting for half an hour, our skirmishers announced another charge and the men stood, or knelt rather, to their guns. On the rebels came, through the woods, straight against Bidwell's line and the left of Grant's, with a vigor that promised success. As they pressed us harder and harder, the lines being but a few yards apart, Bidwell's brigade began doggedly to give way, gradually retreating step by step almost to the foot of our little hill, of which the rebels now occupied the summit, while the left regiments of Grant also swung back, without confusion, to maintain the continuity of the line. A panic for a moment seemed to threaten the Sixth and Eleventh Vermont, but the bravery of the officers at once restored the courage of the men, and they gave and took without further flinching, though the struggle was deadly. At this critical juncture a shell struck General Bidwell as he sat on his horse, holding his men to their work; he was a man of remarkably large frame, and the missile tore through his shoulders and lungs, bringing him heavily to the ground. Wonderful to relate he lived until evening, and died rejoicing at our victory. He is well remembered by every member of our brigade, which had fought at his side for years, and he was so much beloved and respected by his own men that it seemed impossible but that they would now give up the contest, when Lieut.-Col. French of the Seventy-seventh New York, next in command, shouted, "Don't run till the Vermonters do!" and with a cheer of desperation his troops sprang forward reaching their first position on the crest. The astonished rebels formed in rows behind the trees for protection, and these files were forced to swing first to the east and then to the west as a fire was poured upon them from our Brigade or Colonel French's, until strange as it may appear, many of them actually surrendered themselves as prisoners; two of these were killed together, far behind our line, by the same rebel shell.

Thus our position was for the second time left unvexed. At about this time, General Getty learned of the serious wound of General Ricketts, which left him in command of the Corps. He therefore turned over the Division to General Grant, though he still watched its movements, the First and Third Divisions being far out of reach, no longer "confronting the enemy." Lieutenant Colonel Amasa S. Tracy of the Second Vermont was now in command of the Brigade as its senior officer, Colonel Foster not having as yet come in from the picquet line.

The two repulses thus inflicted upon the enemy must have annoyed him terribly; he had previously routed all the rest of our infantry and had good reason to expect no further labor but pursuit. The attack was at once resumed however, this time upon Warner more especially, though involving our right regiments somewhat. They were checked for a time, and on the next morning the slaughter of rebels in front of this position was seen to have been terrible. But their whole army was now up; we could see heavy columns marching upon the cavalry on our left, while Warner was struck upon his unprotected flank, and a line of rebels even came upon his rear. At this time, Early having now men enough in position to bag our stubborn little Division entire if we longer maintained our stubborness, General Getty sent word to Grant to withdraw unless he saw some especial reason for remaining. The order was handsomely executed. A full line of rebels took possession of our hill almost the very moment we left it, but for some reason they did not see fit to pursue us except with scattering bullets. After retiring about half a mile we halted in an old road just west of Middletown, where we remained for perhaps twenty minutes. Not finding other troops in the vicinity however, and the position being of no value, Grant threw forward Captain Wales with the Second Vermont as skirmishers to cover our retreat, and the Division coolly marched in line of battle a mile further to the rear, when we found a position that General Getty considered suitable to form upon. We therefore faced to the front again while he ordered the other Divisions, then still further to the rear, to conform to the movements of his own.

It was then about 10 A. M., and Early now lost the opportunity which might have given him complete success. In the night after this same day, General Sheridan's cavalry pursued the routed enemy to New Market without a halt, but Early, after his victory of the morning, kindly gave us three valuable hours in which to reform our scattered troops, without attempting to prevent it. A General Order which he subsequently published to his troops, recognizes his failure to properly push his success, and says he was unable to give the rapid pursuit he desired, because his men had so generally left their ranks to plunder our deserted camps and rifle the pockets of our dead and wounded. The blame rests upon himself, for it was truly a sad state of discipline which could not keep together, in the flush of victory, a sufficient number of men to follow up a disorganized retreat; his gallant army was not alone in fault for this shameful state of affairs which he reprobates so bitterly. And even if his infantry were beyond his control, where was his large cavalry force, which had not fired a gun except in their insignificant skirmish with our picquets in the early morning? Without doubt the report was correct, which attributed to some of General Early's brilliant young subordinates the inception of the wonderful plan, which it is certain he left to them to execute, and its success, which his own feeble authority and lack of energy were by his own confession entirely incompetent to pursue, or even to preserve.

The position selected by General Getty was behind a long fence, for part of the way a stone wall, stretching west a mile or two from the pike, across ravines, and beyond our own Division extending into a forest. It was evident that we could here check the enemy's next advance, and probably could hold him at bay until he should again outflank us. At the very worst we could make an organized stand and take up an organized retreat. General Wright now devoted himself to arranging the troops on their new line and to our Division belongs the credit of rendering the formation possible. While we had held the hill near Middletown so tenaciously, General Wright had got together the regiments of the Nineteenth Corps and of our First and Third Divisions, and now placed them on our right, forming a strong and defensible line along which a rude protection of earth and rails was at once improvised. He frequently said that he could yet defeat the enemy, and his staff have claimed that he issued orders looking to a counter-attack, but it is doubtful if such a movement would have been successful, as the army was much disheartened. Still we now had an opportunity to rest, and even to breakfast roughly, in a sort of dogged gloom.

French's Brigade now extended from the pike down the hill to Meadow Run; our own Brigade was still in the centre of the Division across the Run, and Warner's on our right. The Third Division followed by the First and the Nineteenth Corps were coming up to prolong our line. Across the pike on the left were two Divisions of cavalry, and Crook's command also there attempted a shadow of a formation, though some of it had already reached Winchester, and the greater part of it was in a fair way to do so soon. A strong and well posted skirmish line again covered our front, which Col. Tracy after Sheridan's arrival rode out on horseback to inspect. As he was reconnoitring with a field glass he was brought to the ground, seriously wounded in his previously unfortunate left leg, and disabled for months.

While thus waiting for the complete re-formation of the army, sulkily and it is to be feared profanely growling over the defeat in detail which we had experienced, though not in the least disposed to admit that our Division had been whipped, in fact a little proud of what we had already done, and expecting the rebel charge which we grew more and more confident we should repulse, we heard cheers behind us on the pike. We were astounded. There we stood, driven four miles already, quietly waiting for what might be further and immediate disaster, while far in the rear we heard the stragglers and hospital bummers, and the gunless artillerymen actually cheering as though a victory had been won. We could hardly believe our ears.

The explanation soon came, in the apparition which

Buchanan Read's as yet embryonic, but now well-known poem, has made familiar. As the sturdy, fiery Sheridan, on his sturdy, fiery steed, flaked with foam from his two hours mad galloping, wheeled from the pike and dashed down the line, our Division also broke forth into the most tumultuous applause. Ardent General Custer first stopped the wonderful Inspirer, and kissed him before his men. His next halt was before our own Brigade. Such a scene as his presence produced and such emotions as it awoke cannot be realized once in a century. All outward manifestations were as enthusiastic as men are capable of exhibiting; cheers seemed to come from throats of brass, and caps were thrown to the tops of the scattering oaks; but beneath and yet superior to these noisy demonstrations, there was in every heart a revulsion of feeling, and a pressure of emotion, beyond description. No more doubt or chance for doubt existed; we were safe, perfectly and unconditionally safe, and every man knew it.

When our greeting had somewhat subsided Col. Tracy, the first man in the Corps to address him, rode up, hat in hand, saying, "General, we're glad to see you." "Well, by G—, I'm glad to be here," exclaimed the General, "What troops are these?" "Sixth Corps! Vermont Brigade!" was shouted from the ranks. His answer was as prompt: "All right! We're all right! We'll have our camps by night!" and he galloped on. So soon had he determined to defeat the enemy. He soon met General Wright and "suggested that we would fight on Getty's line," sending us word meanwhile that Getty's Division had out-done itself that morning.

It was now about noon. The next hour was spent by the General in riding through the whole command, confirming Wright's dispositions and inspiriting the troops by his presence and his words. He thus surveyed the entire field and felt that he was master of the position. General Wright, General Getty and General Grant returned to their commands. Custer's cavalry was again moved by our rear to the right of the army. About one o'clock the Vermont Brigade was hastily taken through the woods to a point in rear of the Nineteenth Corps, where the enemy were pressing, but the attack was easily repulsed without our assistance. Then we returned to a spot where we were concealed from the enemy's view, but from which we could in a moment reach our old position in the line, and where we quietly waited for the order to advance. In ten minutes half the men, with genuine soldier nonchalance, were fast asleep.

Sheridan's plan of battle was something as follows: to throw forward the right, Nineteenth Corps and Cavalry, striking the left of the enemy and turning it if possible; to occupy the rest of his line by a sharp attack but especially to overwhelm his left, the whole army following the movement in a grand left wheel. With this view the Sixth Corps, our left, was drawn up in one line, considerably extended, while the Nineteenth was massed in two lines, its flank weighted by the cavalry.

Time was consumed in making the necessary dispositions and in distributing ammunition, so that it was nearly four o'clock when the few guns we had remaining commenced their usual ante-battle salute. The challenge was promptly answered, and at the appointed time the whole line advanced against the enemy. Their stragglers had been collected, their line was well closed up and strongly posted, and their advance would soon have been resumed, had not our army taken the initiative. The long thin line of the Sixth Corps was thus hurled against a very heavy line of the enemy, covered throughout by a series of stone walls.

Our own Division was now the only one in our sight, the rest of the battle commencing in the woods. So it happened that as French's Brigade on Grant's left, General Bidwell being absent and dying, crossed a long open field into the line of fire that flamed from the wall before them, being ordered to move slowly as the pivot of the army wheel, it staggered and at last fell back to its starting place. Warner's troops on our right had obliqued over a hill where we could no longer see them; we were therefore forced to halt behind a fortunate wall, low, and just long enough to cover our Brigade, where we opened fire. Directly in front of our position were a house, mill, and other out-buildings, swarming with the enemy, our only approach to which was along a narrow road by the side of a little mill-pond formed by a dam across our old annoyance, Meadow Run.

French's broken Brigade seeing that we refused to retire, rallied with very little delay and again advanced to the charge, this time by General Getty's direction on the double quick, its commander having complained that he could not take his men over the open field at a slower pace, and with an apparently unanimous determination to succeed. When they were nearly abreast of our position, being still across the Run, our Brigade poured over the wall which had covered it, and rushed promiscuously into the *cul de sac* by the mill-pond. The attack was successful, and the group of buildings from which the enemy fled in confusion to a wall which protected their second line, was as good a protection for us as it had been for the rebels. The troops of our Brigade were now scattered about the grounds and outbuildings just mentioned, some of them being behind and upon two large hay-stacks, and fully one third of the command being advanced quite a distance further, to the cover of a broken garden wall and among several large trees. French was now in a capital spot nearly up with us, and we were still unable to see the regiments on our right. Officers sent over the hill to reconnoitre found a rebel line of battle and a section of their artillery nearly on the prolongation of our line, and it was considered that we should be doing extremely well if we were able to hold our then position, being it will be remembered the extreme left of the army, with a heavy force of the enemy in our front, and even extending across the pike where we had now no troops except a regiment or so of Col. Kitchen's unattached "provisional" train guard, and some cavalry.

Therefore we kept concealed as much as was consistent with expending the full fifty rounds of ammunition consumed in the next half hour, the rebel fire meanwhile being so hot that we could not carry off our wounded or send for more cartridges. At last however the excellence of Sheridan's plan was proved; a movement became apparent on the right; Warner's left was again seen advancing, and with a cheer we made a final charge against the walls before us. The enemy faced our advance but for a moment and then fled in confusion; we pursued faster and faster, only stopping to hastily fill our cartridge-boxes with captured ammunition; the retreat became a stampede, the pursuit became a reckless chase, and with tumultuous cheers and throbbing hearts we crowded the motley mob before us, on and on over the miles of hill and plain to the banks of Cedar Creek. Our formation was entirely lost but we had the organization and enthusiasm of recognized success; every man felt that it would not do to allow the enemy to rally on this side of the stream; the front was presently occupied by flags alone, as the more heavily loaded troops became unable to keep up with the energetic color-sergeants; the strong cavalry force on our distant right were seen charging down the field; the rebels obliqued confusedly and in uncontrollable dismay towards the turnpike and the bridge; a final attempt was made to organize a last resistance on the hills that crowned the Creek, but after a feeble volley the line melted away; a last battery faced us with a round of canister, but in vain; we saw the flag that followed Sheridan, a white star on the red above a red star on the white, flashing in the front and centre of the army, literally leading it to victory; the regimental standard bearers vied with each other in an eager strife to be first in the works of the morning, every brigade in the army afterwards claiming the distinction, our own brigade certainly not with the least ground of any; and so at last we manned the entrenchments of the Nineteenth Corps, while the foe toiled up the other bank of Cedar Creek and hastily formed a battle-line outside our musket range.

Artillery came up on the gallop and opened vigorously. Generals exchanged congratulations with each other and their troops. Sheridan's promise was fulfilled again, for we had our camps as the evening fell.

It is perhaps not surprising that sarcastic cheers and impudent questions concerning the distance to Harper's Ferry and the probabilities of an early mail saluted a few of Gen. Crook's officers who followed to witness our success. The feeling was prevalent and not unreasonable that we were indebted to them alone for our day's work, with the terrible discomfiture of the morning, but we were afterwards convinced that they had done what they could.

Sheridan was not satisfied even yet. Custer was ordered to pursue the enemy still further. We saw in the twilight the regiments he had selected, being the First Vermont and the Fifth New York Cavalry, cross the creek at a ford a mile above the bridge, then gradually deploy and climb the hill in an extended line; a volley awaited them at its summit which was like a blaze of fire in the darkness, but the brave horsemen did not falter, and that volley was the last.

"Every regiment to its camp of the morning" was

the order next received, and we joyfully picked our way to our first position. Tent poles, rude tables, and rustic couches were found undisturbed; a few minutes more and everything was as it had been twenty-four hours before, save in the absence of the fallen. Fires were lighted and the excited men, though weary, were more ready to discuss and congratulate than to sleep; while once and anon a quiet party would sally forth into the night to find and save some groaning sufferer. The bodies of the Union troops left dead and wounded on the field in our first retreat had been most shamefully plundered by the rebels, many of them lying naked on the ground when recaptured.

At perhaps ten P. M., a cavalry acquaintance hurried into camp and from him we learned the sequel of the day; how Custer and Davies had pushed the cavalry over Fisher's Hill and were still in pursuit; how all our captured cannon had been re-taken and nearly every one of the enemy's guns had been brought into camp by their own unwilling drivers; how prisoners were crowding in by hundreds and the vacant space in front of Sheridan's headquarters had become a corral, full of all sorts of plunder, men, guns, wagons, and mules, upon which he was wont for many days to look with grim satisfaction; how a Vermont boy had, single-handed, captured a rebel General, for which he afterwards received a well-earned decoration, naively telling Secretary Stanton at the time of its bestowal that the Johnnies in the darkness expostulated with him for interfering with "the General's" ambulance, whereat he "guessed the

General was the very man he was looking for;" how in fact the turnpike had been blocked at the foot of Fisher's Hill, and three miles of wagons and guns were captured entire.

The defeat was utter, and decisive so far as the Shenandoah Valley was concerned. Its secret was simply Sheridan's personal magnetism, and all-conquering energy. He felt no doubt, he would submit to no defeat, and he took his army with him as on a whirlwind.

General Grant well said with generous eulogy, "this victory stamps Sheridan as what I have always thought him, one of the ablest of Generals."

It was announced in another vivid dispatch as follows:

"OCTOBER 19th, 10 P.M.

LIEUTENANT GENERAL GRANT:

I have the honor to report that my army at Cedar Creek was attacked this morning before daylight, and my left was turned and driven in confusion. In fact most of the line was driven in confusion with the loss of 20 pieces of artillery. I hastened from Winchester where I was on my return from Washington and found the armies between Middletown and Newtown, having been driven back about four miles. I here took the affair in hand, and quickly united the corps, formed a compact line of battle just in time to repulse an attack of the enemy which was handsomely done at about one P. M.; at 3 P. M., after some changes of the cavalry from the left to the right, I attacked with great vigor, capturing, according to the last report, 43 pieces of artillery, with very many prisoners. I do not know yet the number of my casualties or the losses of the enemy.

Wagon trains, ammunition and caissons in large abundance are in our possession. General Ramseur is a prisoner in our hands, severely and perhaps mortally wounded. I have to report the loss of Gen. Bidwell, killed, and Generals Wright, Grover and Ricketts wounded. Wright is slightly wounded. Affairs at times looked badly, but by the gallantry of our brave officers and men disaster has been converted into a splendid victory. Darkness again intervened to shut off greater results. I now occupy Strasburg.

P. H. SHERIDAN,
Maj.-Gen.

And again on the 21st:

* * * "The accident in the morning turned to our advantage, as much as though the whole thing had been planned." * * * * * * * * * * * *

The actual number of cannon captured was 53 including those lost in the morning; we also took 1100 prisoners besides the enemy's wounded, with which the village of Strasburg was crowded.

Major General Wright's official report proposes the following explanation of the surprise of Crook's command:

"A brigade sent out by General Crook on the preceding day to ascertain the position of the enemy had returned to camp and reported that nothing was to be found in the old camps of the enemy and that he had doubtless retreated up the Valley. * * * * * * However this mistake was made, I have no question that the belief in the retreat of the enemy was generally entertained throughout the reconnoitring force."

"This force, which as before remarked was from the army of West Virginia, returned to camp through its own lines and must have made known to the troops in camp and on the picket line its received belief in the enemy's retreat. Now it happens that the advance of the enemy was made upon this part of the line; the surprise was complete, for the pickets did not fire a shot, and the first indication of the enemy's presence was a volley into the main line where the men of part of the regiments were at reveille roll call without arms. As the entire picket line over that part crossed by the enemy was captured without a shot being fired, no explanation could be obtained from any of the men comprising it; but it is fair to suppose that they were lulled into an unusual security by the report of the previous evening that the enemy had fallen back, and that there was consequently no danger to be apprehended. This supposition seems to me likely enough; it certainly goes far toward explaining how an enemy in force passed and captured a strong and well connected picket line of old soldiers, without occasioning alarm, and gave as a first warning of its presence a volley of musketry into the main line of unarmed soldiers. It was reported in camp, as derived from the enemy, that he first relieved a part of our line by his own men dressed in our uniforms; but I have never been able to confirm this rumor."

General Sheridan says, "This surprise was owing, probably, to not closing in Powell," who was towards Front Royal, rather than watching the nearer fords, "or that the Cavalry Divisions of Merritt and Custer were placed on the right of our line, where it had always occurred to me there was but little danger of an attack."

These two hypotheses are both doubtless correct, General Sheridan proposing the more remote strategical error, while Wright explains the more immediate carelessness which enabled the enemy to surprise Crook's camp, without notice from his picquets.

General Wright's report continues: "The proceedings up to this point were bad enough for us, as it gave the enemy, almost without a struggle, the entire left of our line, with considerable artillery, not a gun of which had fired a shot. But the reserve of this line was posted a considerable distance in its rear, where it could be made available as a movable force, and was well situated to operate upon any force attempting to turn our left. It was in no way involved in the disaster of the first line, which was after all but a small part of our whole force, being only one weak division; and its loss was in no wise to be taken as deciding the fate of the day; with the other troops brought up, this supporting division was in good position to offer sturdy battle with every prospect of repulsing the enemy; and aided as it would have been by the rest of the army, the chances were largely in our favor. Here the battle should have been fought and won; and long before mid-day the discomfitted enemy should have been driven across Cedar Creek, stripped of all the captures of his first attack. But from some unexplainable cause the troops forming this part of the line would not stand, but broke under a scattered fire which should not have occasioned the slightest apprehension in raw recruits, much less in old soldiers like themselves. Most officers who have served through the war have had instances of the same kind in their own experience, and will therefore perfectly understand this, though they may find themselves as much at a loss for a satisfactory explanation of its cause."

"It was the breaking of this line which involved the necessity of falling back; a change of front was necessary, and this must be made to a position which would place our force between the enemy and our base. That there was no intention of retreating, the soldiers who stood firm clearly understood, and when once brought into the new position in face of the enemy they were ready to advance upon him as was shown by their magnificent attack when ordered forward."

"To the Sixth Corps which it was my honor to command after the death of that noble soldier Sedgwick,—to its officers and men, I desire to acknowledge the obligations which in addition to the many others it has imposed, it laid upon the country by its steadiness, courage and discipline in this important battle: without disparagement to the soldierly qualities of other organizations concerned, it is but just to claim for it a large share in the successes of the day. Being from the nature of the attack upon our lines somewhat in the position of a reserve force, and therefore fairly to be called upon to turn the tide of unsuccessful battle, it came up nobly to its duty, fully sustaining its former well earned laurels."

General Getty's official report contains the following paragraph:

"I take just pride in recapitulating the services of the Division on this eventful day. At daybreak the Division was on the extreme right of the infantry of the army. Immediately after daylight it moved by the left toward Middletown with a view of gaining possession of the pike and the high ground near the town. On its march it encountered the enemy, formed line rapidly, and immediately advanced, driving the enemy, and taking some prisoners, at this time finding itself on the extreme left. Compelled from unforeseen causes to halt and occupy a crest 300 yards to the rear, it held this position unsupported for over an hour after all other troops had left the field, checking the further advance of the enemy and repulsing every attack, thus giving time to the scattered commands to reorganize and reform. Finally outnumbered and outflanked, the Division moved back leisurely, contesting every inch of ground, about a mile to the north of Middletown, with its left resting on the pike, and in this position served as the nucleus on which the lines of the army were reformed. In the afternoon the Division advanced upon the lines of the enemy, over almost entirely open ground, in the face of a heavy fire of musketry and artillery; and although parts of the line had to yield for the moment to the galling fire encountered, the mass of the Division moved steadily on, driving the enemy from his first position back upon his second, and eventually forcing him from this position and driving him in confusion through Middletown and the plains beyond, to and over Cedar Creek."

The following table shows the casualties of the Brigade at the battle of Cedar Creek, as first reported:

REGIMENT.	KILLED.	WOUNDED.	MISSING.	TOTAL.
2d.	3	31	4	38
3d.	3	38	1	42
4th.	6	20	3	29
5th.	2	17	3	22
6th.	5	32	11	48
11th.	9	74	29	112
Aggregate,	28	212	51	291

The prisoners it will be remembered were lost from the picquet line at daybreak. A subsequent revision corrected this aggregate as follows: killed 33, wounded 210, missing 41, total 284.

The only officer killed was Second Lieutenant Oscar R. Lee, of the Eleventh Regiment. He was a remarkably brave and efficient officer, from Waterford, whose commission as Captain was received a few days after his death. A commission previously issued to Lieutenant Duhigg as Captain of the same company (M) had in like manner reached the regiment a day or two after that officer was killed at the Opequan.

Captain Edward P. Lee, a brother of Lieutenant Lee and in the same Regiment, was among the wounded. The other officers wounded were Lieutenant Colonel Tracy and Lieutenant Amasa W. Ferry of the Second; Captain William H. Hubbard and Lieutenant Augustus H. Lyon of the Third; Captain Joseph P. Aikens of the Fourth; Captain Thomas Kavanaugh of the Fifth; Captain Edwin R. Kinney and Captain Thomas B. Kennedy of the Sixth, Captain Kinney being the senior officer of his Regiment and succeeded in command by Captain Sperry after receiving his wound; Lieutenant George O. French of the Eleventh, afterwards killed at Petersburg, together with Captain George H. Amidon of the Fourth, and Lieutenant Henry C. Baxter of the Eleventh who were serving on the Brigade Staff.

XIII.

CONCLUSION.

But little worth the writing now remains of my subject. The Shenandoah Valley was fairly and finally conquered and a season of rest ensued, varied only by the ordinary incidents of life in camp, and rumors, which had grown to be stale and profitless by frequent repetition, of our expected removal to Petersburg and the army of the Potomac.

On the 21st of October, our Division then still on the extreme left of the army, was transferred to the village of Strasburg, the Vermont Brigade occupying the town itself, and finding capital quarters. The rest of the army still held the north bank of Cedar Creek, while we acted as a grand guard with our outposts on Fisher's Hill. We were entirely unmolested during the fortnight we spent there, and were made happy by an opportunity to renew our acquaintance with Paymaster Hayward and his greenbacks.

There being no further signs of an enemy, the army presently moved back to Kernstown, a few miles south of Winchester; the railroad being soon put in running order from Harper's Ferry to Stevenson's Depot, but six miles from camp, we were again at our base and accessible to military comforts. Hay for the horses was issued for the first time since the army of the Potomac had crossed the Rapidan in May, while suttlers began anew to vend their salt mackerel and clammy gingerbread.

The presidential election was held, the Brigade again having an opportunity to vote and casting a large majority for Abraham Lincoln, though some of the veterans of the peninsula still had sufficient enthusiasm for McClellan to honor him with their ballots.

Evening dress-parades and formal guard-mountings were resumed. Gen. Getty each morning collected together the guards and picquets of the Division, and thus made a remarkably fine display of the most interesting ceremony of the Regulations, while the evening parades were by Brigades, our own of course conducted by General Grant.

On the 21st of November the Corps was reviewed by General Sheridan. It turned out in large numbers and in fine style, and the sight would have been an exceedingly imposing one, had not a blustering rain set in which converted the field into a sea of mud and dampened all enthusiasm. Still it was an admirable performance, and it may be doubted if the steadiness of marching shown has ever been equalled by so large a number of troops upon our continent.

The 24th was Thanksgiving day at home, and was remembered in camp. The weather was beautiful, all drills and labor were suspended, barrels of turkeys and other good things had been forwarded from the north, which were faithfully distributed among the men ; and Vermont, where we hoped, yet somewhat doubtfully, to spend our next Thanksgiving, was the universal subject of conversation and field of fancy. The "loved ones at home" during the war doubtless spent much time in pitying the soldiers and longing for their return, while suffering deeply from their absence and danger, but one misery they were spared, they could not be homesick; while the "boys in the field" were many of them afflicted with chronic nostalgia except on letter days.

The campaign now closed had been a hard but a pleasant one. It commenced when the men were exhausted with the unprecedented labor imposed upon the army of the Potomac in its progress from the Rapidan to Petersburg, comprising two months of continuous fighting, relieved only by most wearisome marches and labor in the trenches. The investment of Petersburg was just completed when we were called away, and entered at once in the heat of the summer upon another month of the most severe marching, and fatiguing campaigning, that we had ever been called upon to perform. At the beginning of August when Hunter was relieved we were as well nigh exhausted as men could be and still retain any energy to be, or to do, or to suffer. From Sheridan's arrival our case began to mend. The weather grew cooler; the marches were easier; we were presently successful in battle; and at last, at the termination of the season we were in the best possible condition, contented with ourselves and proud of our services, with small sick-lists and plenty of supplies, preparing winter-quarters, ready for any movement, though hoping to the last against hope that Petersburg would not again be our destination.

Our Brigade was ably served in the Shenandoah, by

its non-combatant staff, whose labors should not be forgotten. The duties of the various Regimental Quartermasters were especially severe on account of the long distance each supply train had to traverse. Martinsburg, where they made their headquarters, was a perfect pandemonium one day in four, mules, wagons, soldiers, negroes and carts being mingled apparently inextricably and almost undistinguishably, while the days when the caravan was on the march were not only tedious but often dangerous, the guerrillas never ceasing to annoy. Captain Randall of the Sixth was the Brigade Quartermaster and was an exceedingly hard working and efficient officer. Lieutenant Clark of the Eleventh was also in charge of that department a portion of the time, and was not surpassed by any officer in his branch of the service in the foresight with which he anticipated every want that could be supplied, and "drew for it."

Capt. Valentine, the Brigade Commissary, supplied our bodily necessities as abundantly as the facilities for transportation would allow.

But among all the faithful soldiers of the Brigade, the one who will be longest remembered with affection by the greatest number and with the greatest reason, is Castanus B. Park of the 11th Regiment, the Brigade Surgeon. As a worker Dr. Park was indefatigable, and his skill was equal to the requirements of his position. Of all its medical staff the Brigade were justly proud, the assistant surgeons as well as the surgeons being always found at their posts, and shrinking from no labor that might benefit their men on the march, in the camp or in battle. Their duties were often extremely arduous, for in case of an engagement the work of the surgeons was but just begun when ours was over. At and after the battle of Cedar Creek Dr. Park was at his table for forty-eight hours consecutively, and during this campaign it was his duty to perform all the capital operations required in the Brigade. The number of amputations which he performed was exceedingly large, but he traced with care the after history of each patient, and in no single instance did one fail of recovery. This fact speaks equally well for the *physique* of the men and for the science of the Doctor.

Among the officers of the Brigade, who were all so gallant in action that their bravery became a proverb—Col. Warner in reporting the battle of the Opequan said that to specify those who had distinguished themselves would be to give a complete roster of the commissioned officers of the Brigade—the following were honored with brevets for "meritorious services" during this campaign, receiving commissions signed by the President according them Brevet rank as follows:

In the 2d Regiment.	Enoch E. Johnson, Lieutenant Colonel. Elijah Wales, Major. Erastus G. Ballou, Major.
In the 3d Regiment.	Horace W. Floyd, Colonel.
In the 4th Regiment.	George P. Foster, Brigadier General.
In the 11th Regiment.	James M. Warner, Brigadier General. Aldace F. Walker, Lieutenant Colonel. James E. Eldridge, Major. Henry C. Baxter, Captain.

Many of these officers were afterwards advanced to the full rank of their brevets.

The Vermont Brigade was one of the last in the corps to return to Petersburg. On the 9th of December, in a driving snow-storm, it took the cars at Stevenson's depot, and thus, in the night and the tempest it finally left the Shenandoah Valley.

The muster-rolls of the Vermont Brigade enable the author to give the names of its members who were killed or mortally wounded in the Shenandoah Valley. His little book, dedicated to their memory, would be incomplete without such a record. It should be observed, however, that the remark on the rolls, "died of wounds received in action," opposite the names of those not instantly killed, does not contain exact information as to the time the fatal injury was received. The date of death, however, is always given, so that the following list can be relied upon as substantially correct. Persons having knowledge either of omissions or of names improperly inserted are requested to suggest corrections.

The lists are arranged alphabetically, without titles. Rank is no longer of consequence to them, and their fellow citizens hold the memory of all in equal estimation.

DIED

OF WOUNDS RECEIVED IN ACTION, IN THE SHENANDOAH CAMPAIGN

1864.

SECOND REGIMENT.

Jonathan Camp, Wells Howard, Charles H. Stowe,
Henry M. Clark, Benjamin F. Hurlburd, James C. Sweetzer,
Marcus M. Clough, James C. Hutchinson, Jonathan E. Tupper,
Clark Curtice, John B. Lute, James A. Walcott,
Dexter Crossman, Michael Lynch, Arthur Ward,
Alonzo H. Fields, Thomas McGelley, Lewis H. Welcome.
Zenas Hatch, William Reed,

THIRD REGIMENT.

Joseph Blanshaw, James Greig, Charles H. Sanborn,
Eliphalet B. Crane, John S. Kilby, Daniel E. Smith,
John A. Deady, Thomas J. Miller, Elbridge G. Thompson,
Charles Gee, Myron E. Parker, Henry C. Vroody.
Austin Goodell, John J. Rich,

FOURTH REGIMENT.

Kneeland Badger, Lawrence Edwards, Joseph Marson,
Charles A. Blanchard, Caros O. Gibson, Smith Ormsbee,
Zaccheus Blood, James Gill, Richard F. Rich,
Thomas J. Burnham, Napoleon B. Hudson, Luther B. Scott,
Charles Camp, Nelson D. Knight, Ransom W. Towle.

FIFTH REGIMENT.

Joseph Blair, Woodman Jackman, John Naylor,
Lewis Bonett, Peter Ladam, Addison Whitcomb,
Gilbert E. Davis, Julius Lewis, William P. Valentine.
Joseph Farnum,

SIXTH REGIMENT.

Thomas Alden,	Alvah M. Gray,	Edwin R. Richardson,
John Betney,	Edwin Gray,	Alden A. Spaulding,
Charles Blake,	John P. How,	Sylvester Spooner,
Warren H. Chapman,	Claphas Jenno,	Alden Thomas,
Lewis B. Cook,	John Kelley,	Lewis A. Tyler,
Daniel Call,	Samuel Leazar,	Charles P. Upham,
Augustus L. Cox,	Warren D. Mather,	Thomas S. Varney,
Simon P Dean,	Edward Morse,	Joseph Vondell,
Carlos W. Dwinell,	Charles Parmenter,	Stephen P. White.
John Fitzsimmons,	Leander Poquet,	

ELEVENTH REGIMENT.

John S. Andrews,	Daniel B. Field,	Julius Minor,
George F. Bates.	John H. Fisk,	Ransom M. Patch,
Manley E. Bellus,	Orson G. Gibson,	George A. Peeler,
Wyman R. Burnap,	Allen W. Goodrich,	Edgar M. Phinney,
Charles Buxton,	Levi L. Goodrich,	Joseph Rabiteaux,
Clesson Cameron,	David Goosey,	Marcellus Russell,
George R. Campbell,	Obed S Hatch,	Wesley G. Sheldon,
Joel W. Chafee,	George L. Heath,	Nelson F. Skinner,
George E. Chamberlin,	George T. Kasson,	Robert Tibbetts,
John Copeland,	George A. Kilmer,	Foster Thomas,
Stephen Currier,	Erastus Laird,	Ira C. Tompkins,
Willard M. Davis,	Oscar R. Lee,	Ira C. Twiss,
Henry E Decamp,	Myron A. Locklin,	Albert Witherbee,
Charles Devereux,	Elbridge F. Lynde,	John D. Williams,
Charles Doolittle,	John McCarty,	Marshall Wilmarth,
Dennis Duhigg,	Joseph McLaughlin,	Albert Woodworth,
Lyman Dunbar,	Frank Minor,	John Woodward.
Benjamin S. Edgerton,		

THE SHENANDOAH CAMPAIGN.

MAJOR-GENERAL SHERIDAN'S REPORT.

HEADQUARTERS MILITARY DIVISION OF THE GULF,
NEW ORLEANS, February 3, 1866.

Brevet Major-General J. A. Rawlins, Chief of Staff, Washington, D. C.

GENERAL—I have the honor to make the following report of the campaign in the Valley of the Shenandoah, commencing August fourth, 1864.

On the evening of the first of August I was relieved from the command of the cavalry corps of the Army of the Potomac, to take command of the Army of the Shenandoah, and on arriving at Washington on the fourth instant I received directions from Major-General H. W. Halleck, Chief of the Staff, to proceed without delay to Monocacy Junction, on the Baltimore and Ohio railroad, and report in person to the Lieutenant-General. At Monocacy the Lieutenant-General turned over to me the instructions which he had previously given to Major General Hunter, commanding the Department of West Virginia, a copy of which is herewith attached.

The Army of the Shenandoah at this time consisted of the Sixth corps, very much reduced in numbers, one division of the Nineteenth corps, two small infantry divisions under command of General Crook, afterwards designated as the Army of West Virginia, a small division of cavalry under General Averell, which was at that time in pursuit of General McCausland, near Moorefield, McCausland having made a raid into Pennsylvania and burned the town of Chambersburg; there was also one small division of cavalry, then arriving at Washington, from my old corps.

The infantry portion of these troops had been lying in bivouac in the vicinity of Monocacy Junction and Frederick City, but had been ordered to march the day I reported, with directions to concentrate at Halltown, four miles in front of Harper's Ferry. After my interview with the Lieutenant-General, I hastened to Harper's Ferry to make preparations for an immediate advance against the enemy, who then occupied Martinsburg, Williamsport, and Shepardstown, sending occasional raiding parties as far as Hagerstown. The concentration of my command at Halltown alarmed the enemy, and caused him to concentrate at or near Martinsburg, drawing in all his parties from the north side of the Potomac. The indications were that he had intended another raid into Maryland, prompted perhaps by the slight success he had gained over General Crook's command at Kernstown, a short time before. The city of Martinsburg, at which the enemy concentrated, is on the Baltimore and Ohio railroad, at the northern terminus of the valley pike, a broad macadamized road running up the valley, through Winchester, and terminating at Staunton. The Shenandoah valley is a continuation of the Cumberland valley, south of the Potomac, and is bounded on the east by the Blue Ridge, and on the west by the eastern slope of the Alleghany mountains, the general direction of these chains being south-west.

The valley at Martinsburg is about sixty miles broad, at Winchester forty to forty-five, and at Strasburg twenty-five to thirty miles, where an isolated chain, called Massanutten mountain, rises up running parallel to the Blue Ridge, and terminates at Harrisonburg; here the valley again opens out fifty or sixty miles broad. This isolated chain divides the valley, for its continuance, into two valleys, the one next the Blue Ridge being called the Luray valley, the one west of it the Strasburg or main valley. The Blue Ridge has many passes through it called gaps, the principal ones and those which have good wagon roads, are Snicker's, Ashby's, Manassas, Chester, Thoroughfare, Swift Run, Brown's, Rock-fish, and two or three others from the latter one up to Lynchburg. Many have macadamized roads through them, and, indeed, are not gaps, but small valleys through the main chain. The general bearing of all these roads is towards Gordonsville, and are excellent for troops to move upon from that point into the valley; in fact, the Blue Ridge can be crossed almost anywhere by infantry or cavalry.

The valley itself was rich in grain, cattle, sheep, hogs and fruit, and was in such a prosperous condition that the rebel army could march down and up it, billeting on the inhabitants. Such, in brief, is the outline, and was the condition of the Shenandoah valley when I entered it August fourth, 1864.

Great exertions were made to get the troops in readiness for an advance, and on the morning of August tenth, General Torbert's division of cavalry having joined me from Washington, a forward movement was commenced. The enemy, while we were making our preparations, took position at Bunker Hill and vicinity, twelve miles south of Martinsburg, frequently pushing his scouting parties through Smithfield and up to Charlestown. Torbert was ordered to move on the Berryville pike, through Berryville, and go into position near White Post; the Sixth corps moved *via* the Charlestown and Summit Point road to Clifton; the Nineteenth corps moved on the Berryville pike, to the left of the position of the Sixth corps at Clifton; General Crook's command *via* Kabletown, to the vicinity of

Berryville, coming into position on the left of the Nineteenth corps; and Colonel Lowell, with two small regiments of cavalry, was ordered to Summit Point; so that on the night of August tenth, the army occupied a position stretching from Clifton to Berryville, with cavalry at White Post and Summit Point. The enemy moved from vicinity of Bunker Hill, stretching his line from where the Winchester and Potomac railroad crosses Opequan creek, to where the Berryville and Winchester pike crosses the same stream, occupying the west bank. On the morning of August eleventh, the Sixth corps was ordered to move from Clifton across the country to where the Berryville pike crosses Opequan creek, carry the crossing, and hold it; the Nineteenth corps was directed to move through Berryville, on the White Post road, for one mile, file to the right by heads of regiments, at deploying distances, and carry and hold the crossing of Opequan creek at a ford about three-fourths of a mile from the left of the Sixth corps; Crook's command was ordered to move out on the White Post road, one mile and a half beyond Berryville, file to the right and secure the crossing of Opequan creek at a ford about one mile to the left of the Nineteenth corps; Torbert was directed to move with Merritt's division of cavalry up the Millwood pike toward Winchester, attack any force he might find, and, if possible, ascertain the movements of the rebel army. Lowell was ordered to close in from Summit Point on the right of the Sixth corps.

My intention in securing these fords was to march on Winchester, at which point, from all my information on the tenth, I thought the enemy would make a stand. In this I was mistaken, as the results of Torbert's reconnoissance proved. Merritt found the enemy's cavalry covering the Millwood pike west of the Opequan, and, attacking it, drove it in the direction of Kernstown, and discovered the enemy retreating up the valley pike.

As soon as this information was obtained, Torbert was ordered to move quickly, *via* the toll gate on the Front Royal pike, to Newtown, to strike the enemy's flank, and harass him in his retreat, and Lowell to follow up through Winchester. Crook was turned to the left and ordered to Stony Point, or Nineveh, while Emory and Wright were marched to the left, and went into camp between the Millwood and Front Royal pikes, Crook encamping at Strong Point. Torbert met some of the enemy's cavalry at the toll gate on the Front Royal pike, drove it in the direction of Newtown, and behind Gordon's division of infantry, which had been thrown out from Newtown to cover the flank of the main column in its retreat, and which had put itself behind rail barricades. A portion of Merritt's cavalry attacked this infantry, and drove in its skirmish line, and although unable to dislodge the division, held all the ground gained. The rebel division during the night moved off. Next day Crook moved from Stony Point to Cedar creek, Emory followed; the cavalry moved to the same point, *via* Newtown and the valley pike, and the Sixth corps followed the cavalry. On the night of the twelfth, Crook was in position at Cedar creek, on the left of the valley pike, Emory on the right of the pike, the Sixth corps on the right of Emory, and the cavalry on the right and left flanks. A heavy skirmish line was thrown to the heights on the south side of Cedar creek, which had brisk skirmishing during the evening with the enemy's pickets; his (the enemy's) main force occupying the heights above and north of Strasburg. On the morning of the thirteenth, the cavalry was ordered on a reconnoissance towards Strasburg, on the middle road, which road is two and a half miles to the west of the main pike.

Reports of a column of the enemy moving up from Culpepper Court-house, and approaching Front Royal through Chester gap, having been received, caused me much anxiety, as any considerable force advanced through Front Royal, and down the F. R. and W. pike toward Winchester, could be thrown in my rear, or, in case of my driving the enemy to Fisher's hill, and taking position in his front, this same force could be moved along the base of Massanutten mountain on the road to Strasburg, with the same result.

As my effective line of battle strength at this time was about eighteen thousand infantry, and thirty-five hundred cavalry, I remained quiet during the day—except the activity on the skirmish line—to await further developments. In the evening the enemy retired with his main force to Fisher's hill. As the rumors of an advancing force from the direction of Culpepper kept increasing, on the morning of the fourteenth I sent a brigade of cavalry to Front Royal, to ascertain definitely, if possible, the truth of such reports, and at the same time crossed the Sixth corps to the south side of Cedar creek and occupied the heights above Strasburg. Considerable picket firing ensued. During the day I received from Colonel Chipman, of the Adjutant-General's office, the following despatch, he having ridden with great haste from Washington through Snicker's gap, escorted by a regiment of cavalry, to deliver the same. It at once explained the movement from Culpepper, and on the morning of the fifteenth, the remaining two brigades of Merritt's division of cavalry were ordered to the crossing of the Shenandoah river near Front Royal, and the Sixth corps withdrawn to the north side of Cedar creek, holding at Strasburg a strong skirmish line.

(By telegraph, received in cypher.)

CITY POINT, August 12, 1864, 9 A. M.

Major-General Halleck:

Inform General Sheridan that it is now certain two divisions of infantry have gone to Early, and some cavalry and twenty pieces of artillery. This movement commenced last Saturday night, he must be cautious, and act now on the defensive until movements here force them to this—to send this way.

Early's force, with this increase, cannot exceed forty thousand men, but this is too much for General Sheridan to attack. Send General Sheridan the remaining brigade of the Nineteenth corps.

I have ordered to Washington all the one hundred day men. Their time will soon be out, but, for the present, they will do to serve in the defense.

U. S. GRANT,
Lieutenant-General.

The receipt of this despatch was very important to me, as I possibly would have remained in uncertainty as to the character of the force coming in on my flank and rear, until it attacked the cavalry, as it did on the sixteenth.

I at once looked over the map of the valley for a defensive line (that is, where a smaller number of troops could hold a greater number) and could see but one such. I refer to that at Halltown, in front of Harper's Ferry. Subsequent experience has convinced me that no other really defensive line exists in the Shenandoah valley. I therefore determined to move back to Halltown, carry out my instructions to destroy forage and subsistence, and increase my strength by Grover's division of the Nineteenth corps, and Wilson's division of cavalry, both of which were marching to join me, *via* Snicker's gap. Emory was ordered to move to Winchester on the night of the fifteenth, and, on the night of the sixteenth, the Sixth corps and Crook's command were ordered to Clifton, *via* Winchester.

On the afternoon of the sixteenth I moved my headquarters back to Winchester; while moving back (at Newtown) I heard cannonading at or near Front Royal, and on reaching Winchester, Merritt's couriers brought despatches from him, stating that he had been attacked at the crossing of the Shenandoah by Kershaw's division of Longstreet's corps, and two brigades of rebel cavalry, and that he had handsomely repulsed the attack, capturing two battle flags and three hundred prisoners. During the night of the sixteenth, and early on the morning of the seventeenth, Emory moved from Winchester to Berryville, and, on the morning of the seventeenth, Crook and Wright reached Winchester and resumed the march toward Clifton; Wright, who had the rear guard, getting only as far as the

Berryville crossing of the Opequan, where he was ordered to remain; Crook getting to the vicinity of Berryville. Lowell reached Winchester with his two regiments of cavalry on the afternoon of the seventeenth, where he was joined by General Wilson's division of cavalry. Merritt, after his handsome engagement near Front Royal, was ordered back to the vicinity of White Post, and General Grover's division joined Emory at Berryville. The enemy having a signal station on Three-top mountain, almost overhanging Strasburg, and from which every movement made by our troops could be seen, was notified early in the morning of the seventeenth as to this condition of affairs, and without delay followed after us, getting into Winchester about sundown, and driving out General Torbert, who was left there with Wilson and Lowell, and the Jersey brigade of the Sixth corps. Wilson and Lowell fell back to Summit Point, and the Jersey brigade joined its corps at the crossing of the Opequan. Kershaw's division, and two brigades of Fitz Lee's cavalry division, which was the force at Front Royal, joined Early at Winchester, I think, on the evening of the seventeenth.

On the eighteenth the Sixth corps moved, *via* Clifton, to Flowing Spring, two miles and a half west of Charlestown, on the Smithfield pike; Emory about two miles and a half south of Charlestown, on the Berryville pike; Merritt came back to Berryville; Wilson remained at Summit Point, covering the crossing of Opequan creek as far north as the bridge at Smithfield; Merritt covering the crossing of the Berryville pike; Crook remained near Clifton, and the next day moved to the left of Emory. This position was maintained until the twenty-first, when the enemy moved a heavy force across the Opequan at the bridge at Smithfield, driving in the cavalry pickets which fell back to Summit Point, and advanced rapidly on the position of the Sixth corps, near Flowing Springs, when a very sharp and obstinate skirmish took place with the heavy picket line of that corps, resulting very much in its favor. The enemy appeared to have thought that I had taken position near Summit Point, and that by moving around rapidly through Smithfield he would get into my rear. In this, however, he was mistaken. During the day Merritt (who had been attacked and held his ground) was recalled from Berryville. Wilson had also been attacked by infantry, and had also held his ground until ordered in. During the night of the twenty-first the army moved back to Halltown without inconvenience or loss; the cavalry, excepting Lowell's command, which formed on the left, moving early on the morning of the twenty-second, and going into position on the right of the line.

On the morning of the twenty-second the enemy moved up

captured, was of so conflicting and contradictory a nature, that I determined to ascertain if possible, while on this defensive line, what reinforcements had actually been received by the enemy. This could only be done by frequent reconnoissances, and their results convinced me that but one division of infantry, Kershaw's, and one division of cavalry, Fitz Lee's, had joined him

On the twenty-third I ordered a reconnoissance by Crook, who was on the left, resulting in a small capture, and a number of casualties to the enemy.

On the twenty-fourth another reconnoissance was made, capturing a number of prisoners, our own loss being about thirty men. On the twenty-fifth there was sharp picket firing during the day on part of the infantry line. The cavalry was ordered to attack the enemy's cavalry at Kearneysville. This attack was handsomely made, but, instead of finding the enemy's cavalry, his infantry was encountered, and for a time doubled up and thrown into the utmost confusion. It was marching towards Shepardstown. This engagement was somewhat of a mutual surprise—our cavalry expecting to meet the enemy's cavalry, and his infantry expecting no opposition whatever. General Torbert, who was in command, finding a large force of the rebel infantry in his front, came back to our left, and the enemy believing his (the enemy's) movements had been discovered, and that the force left by him in my front at Halltown would be attacked, returned in great haste, but, before doing so, isolated Custer's brigade, which had to cross to the north side of the Potomac, at Shepardstown, and join me *via* Harper's Ferry.

For my own part I believed Early meditated a crossing of his cavalry into Maryland, at Williamsport, and I sent Wilson's division around by Harper's Ferry to watch its movements. Averill in the mean time had taken post at Williamsport, on the north side of the Potomac, and held the crossing against a force of rebel cavalry which made the attempt to cross. On the night of the twenty-sixth the enemy silently left my front, moving over Opequan creek, at the Smithfield and Summit Point Crossings, and concentrating his force at Brucetown and Bunker Hill, leaving his cavalry at Leetown and Smithfield.

On the twenty-eighth I moved in front of Charlestown with the infantry, and directed Merritt to attack the enemy's cavalry at Leetown, which he did, defeating it, and pursuing it through Smithfield. Wilson recrossed the Potomac at Shepardstown, and joined the infantry in front of Charlestown.

On the twenty-ninth Averill crossed at Williamsport and advanced to Martinsburg. On the same day two divisions of the enemy's infantry, and a small force of cavalry, attacked Merritt at the Smithfield bridge, and, after a hard fight, drove to Charlestown and pushed well up to my position at Halltown, skirmishing with the cavalry videttes.

The despatches received from the Lieutenant-General commanding, from Captain G. K. Leet, A. A. G., at Washington, and information derived from my scouts, and from prisoners him through Smithfield and back towards Charlestown, the cavalry fighting with great obstinacy until I could reinforce it with Ricketts' division of the Sixth corps, when in turn the enemy was driven back through Smithfield, and over the Opequan, the cavalry again taking post at the Smithfield bridge.

On the thirtieth Torbert was directed to move Merritt and Wilson to Berryville, leaving Lowell to guard the Smithfield bridge and occupy the town.

On the thirty-first Averill was driven back from Martinsburg to Falling Waters.

From the first to the third of September nothing of importance occurred.

On the third, Averill, who had returned to Martinsburg, advanced on Bunker Hill, attacked McCausland's cavalry, defeated it, capturing wagons and prisoners, and destroying a good deal of property. The infantry moved into position stretching from Clifton to Berryville, Wright moving by Summit Point, Crook and Emory by the Berryville pike; Torbert had been ordered to White Post early in the day, and the enemy, supposing that he could cut him off, pushed across the Opequan towards Berryville with Kershaw's division in advance, but this division not expecting infantry, blundered on to Crook's lines about dark, and was vigorously attacked and driven with heavy loss back towards the Opequan. This engagement, which was after nightfall, was very spirited, and our own and the enemy's casualties severe.

From this time until the nineteenth of September I occupied the line from Clifton to Berryville, transferring Crook to Summit Point on the eighth, to use him as a movable column to protect my right flank and line to Harper's Ferry, while the cavalry threatened the enemy's right flank and his line of communications up the valley.

The difference of strength between the two opposing forces at this time was but little.

As I had learned, beyond doubt, from my scouts, that Kershaw's division, which consisted of four brigades, was to be ordered back to Richmond, I had for two weeks patiently waited its withdrawal before attacking, believing the condition of affairs throughout the country required great prudence on my part, that a defeat of the forces of my command could be ill-afforded, and knowing that no interests in the valley, save those of the Baltimore and Ohio railroad, were suffering by the delay. In this view I was coinciding with the Lieutenant-General commanding.

Although the main force remained without change of position from September third to nineteenth, still the cavalry was employed every day in harassing the enemy, its opponents being principally infantry. In these skirmishes the cavalry was becoming educated to attack infantry lines.

On the thirteenth, one of these handsome dashes was made by General McIntosh, of Wilson's division, capturing the Eighth South Carolina regiment at Abram's creek; on the same day Getty's division of the Sixth corps made a reconnoissance to the Opequan, developing a heavy force of the enemy at Edwards' Crossing.

The position which I had taken at Clifton was six miles from Opequan creek, on the west bank of which the enemy was in position. This distance of six miles I determined to hold as my territory by scouting parties, and in holding it in this way, without pushing up the main force, I expected to be able to move on the enemy at the proper time, without his obtaining the information which he would immediately get from his pickets, if I was in close proximity.

On the night of the fifteenth I received reliable information that Kershaw's division was moving through Winchester, and in the direction of Front Royal. Then our time had come, and I almost made up my mind that I would fight at Newtown, on the valley pike, give up my line to the rear, and take that of the enemy. From my position at Clifton I could throw my force into Newtown before Early could get information and move to that point. I was a little timid about this movement until the arrival of General Grant at Charlestown, who endorsed it, and the order for the movement was made out, but, in consequence of a report from General Averill, on the afternoon of the eighteenth of September, that Early had moved two divisions to Martinsburg, I changed this programme, and determined to first catch the two divisions remaining in vicinity of Stevenson's depot, and then the two sent to Martinsburg, in detail. This information was the cause of the battle of Opequan, instead of the battle of Newtown.

At three o'clock on the morning of the nineteenth September the army moved to the attack. Torbert was directed to advance with Merritt's division of cavalry from Summit Point, carry the crossings of Opequan creek, and form a junction at some point near Stevenson's depot with Averill, who moved from Darksville. Wilson was ordered to move rapidly up the Berryville pike from Berryville, carry its crossing of the Opequan, and charge through the gorge or canon, the attack to be supported by the Sixth and Nineteenth corps, both of which moved across the country to the same crossing of the Opequan. Crook moved across the country to be in reserve at the same point.

Wilson, with McIntosh's brigade leading, made a gallant charge through the long canon, and meeting the advance of Ramseur's rebel infantry division, drove it back and captured the earthwork at the mouth of the canon; this movement was immediately followed up by the Sixth corps. The Nineteenth corps was directed, for convenience of movement, to report to General Wright on its arrival at Opequan creek. I followed up the cavalry attack, and selected the ground for the formation of the Sixth and Nineteenth corps, which went into line under a heavy artillery fire.

A good deal of time was lost in this movement through the canon, and it was not until perhaps nine o'clock, A. M., that the order for the advance in line was given. I had, from early in the morning, become apprised that I would have to engage Early's entire army, instead of two divisions, and determined to attack with the Sixth and Nineteenth corps, holding Crook's command as a turning column to use only when the crisis of the battle occurred, and that I would put him in on my left, and still get the valley pike. The attack was therefore made by the Sixth and Nineteenth corps, in very handsome style, and under a heavy fire from the enemy, who held a line which gave him the cover of slight brushwood and cornfields.

The resistance during this attack was obstinate, and, as there were no earthworks to protect, deadly to both sides.

The enemy, after the contest had been going on for some time, made a counter charge, striking the right of the Sixth corps and left of the Nineteenth, driving back the centre of my line.

It was at this juncture that I ordered a brigade of Russell's division of the Sixth corps to wait till the enemy's attacking column presented its flank, then to strike it with vigor. This was handsomely done, the brigade being led by General Russell, and its commander, Upton, in person; the enemy in turn was driven back, our line re-established, and most of the two or three thousand men who had gone to the rear brought back.

I still would not order Crook in, but placed him directly in rear of the line of battle; as the reports, however, that the enemy were attempting to turn my right kept continually increasing, I was obliged to put him in on that flank instead of on the left, as was originally intended. He was directed to act as a turning column, to find the left of the enemy's line, strike it in flank or rear, break it up, and that I would order a left half wheel of the line of battle to support him. In this attack the enemy was driven in confusion from his position, and simultaneous with it Merritt and Averill, under Torbert, could be distinctly seen sweeping up the Martinsburg pike, driving the enemy's cavalry before them in a confused mass through the broken infantry. I then rode along the line of the Nineteenth and Sixth corps, ordered their advance, and directed Wilson, who was on the left flank, to push on and gain the valley pike southof Winchester; after which I returned to the right, where the enemy was still fighting with obstinacy in the open ground in front of Winchester, and ordered Torbert to collect his cavalry and charge, which was done simultaneously with the infantry advance, and the enemy routed.

At daylight on morning of the twentieth of September the army moved rapidly up the valley pike in pursuit of the enemy, who had continued his retreat during the night to Fisher's hill, south of Strasburg.

Fisher's hill is the bluff immediately south of and over a little stream called Tumbling river, and is a position which was almost impregnable to a direct assault, and as the valley is but about three and a half miles wide at this point, the enemy considered himself secure on reaching it, and commenced erecting breastworks across the valley from Fisher's hill to North mountain; so secure, in fact, did he consider himself, that the ammunition boxes were taken from the caissons and placed for convenience behind the breastworks.

On the evening of September twentieth, Wright and Emory went into position on the heights of Strasburg, Crook north of Cedar creek, the cavalry to the right and rear of Wright, and Emory extending to the back road. This night I resolved to use a turning column again, and that I would move Crook, unperceived, if possible, over on to the face of Little North mountain, and let him strike the left and rear of the enemy's line, and then, if successful, make a left half wheel of the whole line of battle to his support. To do this required much secresy, as the enemy had a signal station on Threetop mountain, from which he could see every movement made by our troops; therefore, during the night of the twentieth, I concealed Crook in the timber north of Cedar creek, where he remained during the twenty-first. On the same day I moved Wright and Emory up in the front of the rebel line, getting into proper position after a severe engagement between a portion of Ricketts' and Getty's divisions of the Sixth corps, and a strong force of the enemy. Torbert, with Wilson's and Merritt's cavalry, was ordered down the Luray valley in pursuit of the enemy's cavalry, and, after defeating or driving it, to cross over Luray pike to New Market and intercept the enemy's infantry should I drive it from the position at Fisher's hill.

On the night of the twenty-first, Crook was moved to, and concentrated in, the timber near Strasburg, and at daylight on the twenty-second marched to, and massed in, the timber near Little North mountain. I did not attempt to cover the long front presented by the enemy, but massed the Sixth and Nineteenth corps opposite the right centre of his line. After Crook had gotten into the position last named, I took out Ricketts' division of the Sixth corps and placed it opposite the enemy's left centre, and directed Averill with his cavalry to go up on Ricketts' front and right, and drive in the enemy's skirmish line, if possible. This was done, and the enemy's signal officer on Threetop mountain, mistaking Ricketts' division for my turning column so notified the enemy, and he made his arrangements accordingly, whilst Crook, without being observed, moved on the side of Little North mountain, and struck the enemy's left and rear so suddenly and unexpectedly, that he (the enemy) supposing he must have come across the mountains, broke; Crook swinging down behind the line, Ricketts swinging in and joining Crook, and so on the balance of the Sixth and Nineteenth corps, the rout of the enemy being complete.

Unfortunately the cavalry which I had sent down the Luray valley to cross over to New Market was unsuccessful, and only reached so far as Millford, a point at which the Luray valley contracts to a gorge, and which was taken possession of by the enemy's cavalry in some force. Had General Torbert driven this cavalry, or turned the defile and reached New Market, I have no doubt but that we would have captured the entire rebel army. I feel certain that its rout from Fisher's hill was such that there was scarcely a company organization held together. New Market being at a converging point in the valley they came together again, and to some extent reorganized. I did not wait to see the results of this victory, but pushed on during the night of the twenty-second to Woodstock, although the darkness and consequent confusion made the pursuit slow.

On the morning of September twenty-third, General Devins, with his small brigade of cavalry, moved to a point directly north of Mount Jackson, driving the enemy in his front, and there awaited the arrival of General Averill's division, which for some unaccountable reason went into camp immediately after the battle. General Averill reached Devins' command at three o'clock, P. M., and, in the evening, returned with all the advance cavalry of which he was in command, to a creek one half mile north of Hawkinsburg, and there remained until the arrival of the head of the infantry column, which had halted between Edinburg and Woodstock for wagons, in order to issue the necessary rations.

Early on the morning of the twenty-fourth the entire army reached Mount Jackson, a small town on the north bank of the north fork of the Shenandoah. The enemy had in the mean time reorganized, and taken position on the bluff, south of the river, but had commenced this same morning his retreat toward Harrisonburg; still, he held a long and strong line with the troops that were to cover his rear, in a temporary line of rifle-pits on the bluff commanding the plateau.

To dislodge him from his strong position, Devins' brigade of cavalry was directed to cross the Shenandoah, work around the base of the Massanutten range, and drive in the cavalry which covered his (the enemy's) right flank; and Powell, who had succeeded Averill, was ordered to move around his left flank *via* Simberville, whilst the infantry was rushed across the river by the bridge.

The enemy did not wait the full execution of these movements, but withdrew in haste, the cavalry under Devins coming up with him at Newmarket, and made a bold attempt to hold him until I could push up our infantry, but was unable to do so as the open, smooth country allowed him (the enemy) to retreat with great rapidity in line of battle, and the three or four hundred cavalry under Devins was unable to break this line. Our infantry was pushed by heads of columns very hard to overtake, and bring on an engagement, but could not succeed, and encamped about six miles south of Newmarket for the night.

Powell meantime had pushed on through Simberville, and gained the valley pike near Lacy's springs, capturing some prisoners and wagons.

This movement of Powell's probably forced the enemy to abandon the road *via* Harrisonburg, and move over the Keezeltown road to Port Republic, to which point the retreat was continued through the night of the twenty-fourth, and from thence to Brown's gap in the Blue Ridge.

On the twenty-fifth, the Sixth and Nineteenth corps reached Harrisonburg. Crook was ordered to remain at the junction of the Keezeltown road with the Valley pike until the movements of the enemy were definitely ascertained.

On this day Torbert reached Harrisonburg, having encountered the enemy's cavalry at Luray, defeating it and joining me *via* Newmarket, and Powell had proceeded to Mount Crawford.

On the twenty-sixth Merritt's division of Cavalry was ordered to Port Republic, and Torbert to Staunton and Waynesboro to destroy the bridge at the latter place, and, in retiring, to burn all forage, drive off all cattle, destroy all mills, &c., which would cripple the rebel army or confederacy.

Torbert had with him Wilson's division of cavalry and Lowell's brigade of regulars.

On the twenty-seventh, while Torbert was making his advance on Waynesboro, I ordered Merritt to make a demonstration on Brown's Gap to cover the movement. This brought out the enemy (who had been re-enforced by Kershaw's division which came through Swift Run Gap,) against the small force of cavalry employed in this demonstration, which he followed up to Port Republic, and I believe crossed in some force. Merritt's instructions from me were to resist an attack, but, if pressed, to fall back to Cross Keys, in which event I intended to attack with the main force which was at Harrisonburg, and could be rapidly moved to Cross Keys. The enemy, however, advanced with his main force only to Port Republic, after which he fell back. Torbert this day took possession of Waynesboro, and partially destroyed the railroad bridge, but about dark on the twenty-eighth was attacked by infantry and cavalry, returned to Staunton and from thence to Bridgewater *via* Springhill, executing the order for the destruction of subsistence, forage, &c.

On the morning of the twenty-eighth Merritt was ordered to Port Republic to open communication with General Torbert, but on the same night was directed to leave small forces at Port Republic and Swift-run gap, and proceed with the balance of his command (his own and Custer's divisions) to Piedmont, swing around from that point to near Staunton, burning forage, mills, and such other property as might be serviceable to the rebel army or confederacy, and, on his return, to go into camp on the left of the Sixth and Nineteenth corps, which were ordered to proceed on the twenty-ninth to Mount Crawford, in support of this and Torbert's movements.

September twenty-ninth, Torbert reached Bridgewater, and Merritt Mt. Crawford.

On the first of October Merritt reoccupied Port Republic, and the Sixth and Nineteenth corps were moved back to Harrisonburg.

The question that now presented itself was, whether or not I should follow the enemy to Brown's gap, where he still held fast, drive him out and advance on Charlottesville and Gordonsville. This movement on Gordonsville I was opposed to for many reasons, the most important of which was, that it would necessitate the opening of the Orange and Alexandria railroad from Alexandria, and to protect this road against the numerous guerilla bands, would have required a corps of infantry; besides, I would have been obliged to leave a small force in the valley to give security to the line of the Potomac. This would probably occupy the whole of Crook's command, leaving me but a small number of fighting men. Then there was the additional reason of the uncertainty as to whether the army in front of Petersburg could hold the entire force of General Lee there, and, in case it could not, a sufficient number might be detached and move rapidly by rail and overwhelm me, quickly returning. I was also confident that my transportation could not supply me further than Harrisonburg, and therefore advised that the valley campaign should terminate at

Harrisonburg, and that I return, carrying out my original instructions for the destruction of forage, grain, &c., give up the majority of the army I commanded, and order it to the Petersburg line, a line which I thought the Lieutenant-General believed if a successful movement could be made on, would involve the capture of the Army of Northern Virginia.

I therefore, on the morning of the sixth of October, commenced moving back, stretching the cavalry across the valley from the Blue Ridge to the eastern slope of the Alleghanies, with directions to burn all forage and drive off all stock, &c., as they moved to the rear, fully coinciding in the views and instructions of the Lieutenant-General that the valley should be made a barren waste. The most positive orders were given, however, not to burn dwellings.

In this movement the enemy's cavalry followed at a respectful distance until in the vicinity of Woodstock, when they attacked Custer's division and harassed it as far as Louis brook, a short distance south of Fisher's Hill.

On the night of the eighth, I ordered General Torbert to engage the enemy's cavalry at daylight, and notified him that I would halt the army until he had defeated it.

In compliance with these instructions, Torbert advanced at daylight on the ninth of October, with Custer's division on the back road, and Merritt's division on the Valley pike.

At Louis brook the heads of the opposing columns came in contact and deployed, and after a short but decisive engagement the enemy was defeated, with the loss of all his artillery excepting one piece, and everything else which was carried on wheels. The rout was complete, and was followed up to Mount Jackson, a distance of some twenty-six miles.

On October tenth the enemy crossed to the north side of Cedar creek, the Sixth corps continuing its march to Front Royal; this was the first day's march of this corps to rejoin Lieutenant-General Grant at Petersburg. It was the intention that it should proceed through Manassas gap to Piedmont east of the Blue Ridge—to which point the Manassas gap railroad had been completed, and from thence to Alexandria by rail; but on my recommendation that it would be much better to march it, as it was in fine condition, through Ashby's gap, and thence to Washington, the former route was abandoned, and on the twelfth the corps moved to the Ashby gap crossing of the Shenandoah river; but, on the same day, in consequence of the advance of the enemy to Fisher's Hill, it was recalled to await the development of the enemy's new intentions.

The question now again arose in reference to the advance on Gordonsville, as suggested in the following despatch:

(Cipher.)

WASHINGTON, October 12, 1864, 12 M.

Major-General Sheridan:

Lieutenant-General Grant wishes a position taken far enough south to serve as a base for further operations upon Gordonsville and Charlottesville. It must be strongly fortified and provisioned.

Some point in the vicinity of Manassas gap would seem best suited for all purposes.

Colonel Alexander, of the engineers, will be sent to consult with you as soon as you connect with General Augur.

H. W. HALLECK,
Major-General.

This plan I would not endorse, but, in order to settle it definitely, I was called to Washington by the following telegram:

WASHINGTON, October 13, 1864.

Major-General Sheridan, through General Augur:

If you can come here, a consultation on several points is extremely desirable. I propose to visit General Grant, and would like to see you first.

E. M. STANTON,
Secretary of War.

On the evening of the fifteenth I determined to go, believing that the enemy at Fisher's Hill could not accomplish much; and as I had concluded not to attack him at present, I ordered the whole of the cavalry force under General Torbert to accompany me to Front Royal, from whence I intended to push it through Chester gap to the Virginia Central railroad at Charlottesville, while I passed through Manassas gap to Piedmont, thence by rail to Washington. Upon my arrival with the cavalry at Front Royal, on the night of the sixteenth, I received the following despatch from General Wright, who was left at Cedar Creek in command of the army:

HEADQUARTERS, MIDDLE MILITARY DIVISION,
October 16, 1864.

Major-General P. H. Sheridan, commanding Middle Military Division:

GENERAL—I enclose you despatch which explains itself (see copy following):

If the enemy should be strongly reinforced in cavalry, he might, by turning our right, give us a great deal of trouble. I shall hold on here until the enemy's movements are developed, and shall only fear an attack on my right, which I shall make every preparation for guarding against and resisting.

Very respectfully, your obedient servant,

H. G. WRIGHT,
Major-General Commanding.

To Lieutenant-General Early:

Be ready to move as soon as my forces join you, and we will crush Sheridan.

LONGSTREET,
Lieutenant-General.

This message was taken off the rebel signal flags, on Three Top mountain. My first thought was that it was a ruse, but, on reflection, deemed it best to abandon the cavalry raid, and give to General Wright the entire strength of the army. I therefore ordered the cavalry to return and report to him, and addressed the following note on the subject:

FRONT ROYAL, October 16, 1864.

Major-General H. G. Wright, commanding Sixth Army Corps:

GENERAL—The cavalry is all ordered back to you; make position strong. If Longstreet's despatch is true, he is under the impression that we have largely detached. I will go over to Augur, and may get additional news.

Close in Colonel Powell, who will be at this point. If the enemy should make an advance, I know you will defeat him. Look well to your ground, and be well prepared. Get up everything that can be spared. I will bring up all I can, and will be up on Tuesday, if not sooner.

P. H. SHERIDAN,
Major-General.

After sending this note I continued through Manassas gap and on to Piedmont, and from thence by rail to Washington, arriving on the morning of the seventeenth. At twelve o'clock M. I returned by special train to Martinsburg, arriving on the morning of the eighteenth at Winchester, in company with Colonels Thorn and Alexander, of the Engineer corps, sent with me by General Halleck. During my absence the enemy had gathered all his strength, and, in the night of the eighteenth, and early on the nineteenth, moved silently from Fisher's Hill, through Strasburg, pushed a heavy turning column across the Shenandoah, on the road from Strasburg to Front Royal, and again recrossed the river at Bowman's ford, striking Crook, who held the left of our line, in flank and rear, so unexpectedly and forcibly as to drive in his outposts, invade his camp, and turn his position. This surprise was owing, probably, to not closing in Powell, or that the cavalry divisions of Merritt and Custer were placed on the right of our line, where it had always occurred to me there was but little danger of attack.

This was followed by a direct attack upon our front, and the result was that the whole army was driven back in confusion, to a point about one and a half miles north of Middletown, a very large portion of infantry not even preserving a company organization.

At about seven o'clock on the morning of the nineteenth October, an officer on picket at Winchester reported artillery firing, but, supposing it resulted from a reconnoissance which had been ordered for this morning, I paid no attention to it, and was unconscious of the true position of affairs until about nine o'clock, when, having ridden through the town of Winchester, the sound of the artillery made a battle unmistakable, and on reaching Mill creek, one-half a mile south of Winchester, the head of the fugitives appeared in sight, trains and men coming to the rear with appalling rapidity.

I immediately gave directions to halt and pack the trains at Mill Creek, and ordered the brigade at Winchester to stretch across the country and stop all stragglers. Taking twenty men from my escort, I pushed on to the front, leaving the balance, under General Forsyth and Colonels Thorn and Alexander, to do what they could in stemming the torrent of fugitives.

I am happy to say that hundreds of the men, who on reflection found they had not done themselves justice, came back with cheers.

On arriving at the front, I found Merritt's and Custer's divisions of cavalry, under Torbert, and General Getty's division of the Sixth corps, opposing the enemy. I suggested to General Wright that we would fight on Getty's line, and to transfer Custer to the right at once, as he (Custer) and Merritt, from being on the right in the morning, had been transferred to the left; that the remaining two divisions of the Sixth corps, which were to the right and rear of Getty about two miles, should be ordered up, and also that the Nineteenth corps, which was on the right and rear of these two divisions, should be hastened up before the enemy attacked Getty.

I then started out all my staff officers to bring up these troops, and was so convinced that we would soon be attacked, that I went back myself to urge them on.

Immediately after I returned and assumed command, General Wright returning to his corps, Getty to his division, and the line of battle was formed on the prolongation of General Getty's line, and a temporary breastwork of rails, logs, &c., thrown up hastily.

Shortly after this was done the enemy advanced, and from a point on the left of our line of battle I could see his columns moving to the attack, and at once notified corps commanders to be prepared.

This assault fell principally on the Nineteenth corps, and was repulsed.

I am pleased to be able to state that the strength of the Sixth and Nineteenth corps, and Crook's command, was now being rapidly augmented by the return of those who had gone to the rear early in the day. Reports coming in from the Front Royal pike, on which Powell's division of cavalry was posted, to the effect that a heavy column of infantry was moving on that pike in the direction of Winchester, and that he (Powell) was retiring and would come in at Newtown, caused me great anxiety for the time; and although I could not fully believe that such a movement would be undertaken, still it delayed my general attack.

At four P. M. I ordered the advance. This attack was brilliantly made, and, as the enemy was protected by rail breastworks, and in some portions of his line by stone fences, his resistance was very determined. His line of battle overlapped the right of mine, and by turning with this portion of it on the flank of the Nineteenth corps, caused a slight momentary confusion. This movement was checked, however, by a countercharge of General McMillans' brigade upon the re-entering angle thus formed by the enemy, and his flanking party cut off.

It was at this stage of the battle that Custer was ordered to charge with his entire division; but, although the order was promptly obeyed, it was not in time to capture the whole of the force thus cut off, and many escaped across Cedar creek.

Simultaneous with this charge, a combined movement of the whole line drove the enemy in confusion to the creek, where, owing to the difficulties of crossing, his army became routed.

Custer finding a ford on Cedar creek west of the pike, and Devins, of Merritt's division, one to the east of it, they each made the crossing just after dark, and pursued the routed mass of the enemy to Fisher's Hill, where this strong position gave him some protection against our cavalry; but the most of his transportation had been captured, the road from Cedar creek to Fisher's Hill, a distance of over three miles, being literally blocked by wagons, ambulances, artillery, caissons, &c.

The enemy did not halt his *main* force at Fisher's Hill, but continued the retreat during the night to Newmarket, where his army had, on a similar previous occasion, come together by means of the numerous roads that converge to this point.

This battle practically ended the campaign in the Shenandoah valley. When it opened we found our enemy boastful and confident, unwilling to acknowledge that the soldiers of the Union were their equals in courage and manliness; when it closed with Cedar creek, this impression had been removed from his mind, and gave place to good sense and a strong desire to quit fighting.

The very best troops of the Confederacy had not only been defeated, but had been routed in successive engagements, until their spirit and *esprit* were destroyed; in obtaining these results, however, our loss in officers and men was severe. Practically all territory north of the James river now belonged to me, and the holding of the lines about Petersburg and

Richmond, by the enemy, must have been embarrassing, and invited the question of good military judgment.

On entering the valley it was not my object, by flank movements, to make the enemy change his base, nor to move as far up as the James river, and thus give him the opportunity of making me change *my* base, thereby converting it into a race-course, as heretofore, but to destroy, to the best of my ability, that which was truly the Confederacy—its armies; in doing this, so far as the opposing army was concerned, our success was such that there was no one connected with the army of the Shenandoah who did not so fully realize it as to render the issuing of congratulatory orders unnecessary; every officer and man was made to understand that, when a victory was gained, it was not more than their duty, nor less than their country expected from her gallant sons.

At Winchester, for a moment the contest was uncertain, but the gallant attack of General Upton's brigade of the Sixth corps restored the line of battle, until the turning column of Crook's and Merritt's and Averill's divisions of cavalry, under Torbert, "sent the enemy whirling through Winchester."

In thus particularizing commands and commanders, I only speak in the sense that they were so fortunate as to be available at these important moments.

In the above-mentioned attack by Upton's brigade, the lamented Russell fell. He had been previously wounded, but refused to leave the field. His death brought sadness to every heart in the army.

* * * * * *

At Fisher's Hill it was again the good fortune of General Crook's command to start the enemy, and of General Ricketts' division of the Sixth corps to first gallantly swing in and more fully initiate the rout.

At Cedar creek, Getty's division of the Sixth corps, and Merritt's and Custer's divisions of cavalry, under Torbert, confronted the enemy from the first attack in the morning until the battle was decided, still none behaved more gallantly, or exhibited greater courage than those who returned from the rear, determined to reoccupy their lost camp.

In this engagement, early in the morning, the gallant Colonel Lowell, of the Regular brigade, was wounded while in the advance *en echelon* of Getty's division, but would not leave his command, remaining until the final attack on the enemy was made, in which he was killed.

Generals Bidwell of the Sixth corps, and Thorburn of Crook's command, were also killed in the morning, while behaving with conspicuous gallantry.

I submit the following list of the corps, division, and brigade commanders, who were wounded in the campaign, the killed having already been especially noticed, regretting that the scope of this report will not admit of my specifying by name *all* the many gallant men who were killed and wounded in the numerous engagements in the Shenandoah valley, and most respectfully call attention to the accompanying sub-reports for such particulars as will, I trust, do full justice to all.

Generals H. G. Wright, J. B. Ricketts, Grover, Duval, E. Upton, R. S. McKenzie, Kitchen, (since died of wounds,) J. B. McIntosh, G. H. Chapman, Thomas C. Devins, Penrose, Colonels D. D. Johnson, Daniel McAuley, Jacob Sharpe.

* * * * * *

During this campaign I was at times annoyed by guerilla bands, the most formidable of which was under a partisan chief named Mosby, who made his headquarters east of the Blue Ridge, in the section of country about Upperville. I had constantly refused to operate against these bands, believing them to be substantially a benefit to me, as they prevented straggling, and kept my trains well closed up, and discharged such other duties as would have required a provost guard of at least two regiments of cavalry.

* * * * * *

I attach hereto an abstract of ordnance and ordnance stores captured from the enemy during the campaign (the one hundred and one pieces of artillery being exclusive of the twenty-four pieces recaptured in the afternoon at Cedar creek,) also a detailed report of my casualties, which are in aggregate as follows:

Killed, 1,938; wounded, 11,893; missing, 3,121, total, 16,952.

The records of the Provost Marshal, Middle Military Division, show about thirteen thousand prisoners (as per annexed certificate) to have been received by him, and receipts are among the records of the Assistant Adjutant-General, Middle Military Division, for forty-nine battle-flags, forwarded to the Honorable the Secretary of War.

I am, sir, very respectfully, your obedient servant,

P. H. SHERIDAN,
Major-General U. S. A.

HEADQUARTERS IN THE FIFLD,
MONOCACY RIDGE, MD., August 4, 1864.

Major-General D. Hunter, commanding Department West Virginia.

GENERAL—Concentrate all your available forces without delay in the vicinity of Harper's Ferry, leaving only such railroad guards and garrisons for public property as may be necessary.

Use in this concentration the railroad, if by so doing time can be saved. From Harper's Ferry, if it is found that the enemy has moved north of the Potomac in great force, push north following and attacking him wherever found; following him, if driven south of the Potomac, as long as it is safe to do so. If it is ascertained the enemy has but a small force north of the Potomac, then push south with the main force, detailing, under a competent commander, a sufficient force to look after the raiders, and drive them to their homes.

In detailing such, a force, the brigade of cavalry now *en route* from Washington *via* Rocksville may be taken into account.

There are now on the way to join you three other brigades of the best cavalry, numbering at least five thousand men and horses. These will be instructed, in the absence of further orders, to join you by the south side of the Potomac. One brigade will probably start to-morrow.

In pushing up the Shenandoah valley, as it is expected you will have to go first or last, it is desirable that nothing should be left to invite the enemy to return. Take all provisions, forage, and stock wanted for the use of your command. Such as cannot be consumed, destroy. It is not desirable that buildings should be destroyed, they should rather be protected, but the people should be informed that so long as an enemy can subsist among them, recurrences of these raids must be expected, and we are determined to stop them at all hazards.

Bear in mind the object is to drive the enemy south, and to do this you want to keep him always in sight. Be guided in your course by the course he takes. Make your own arrangements for supplies of all kinds, giving regular vouchers for such as may be taken from loyal citizens.

Very respectfully,

U. S. GRANT,
Lieutenant General.

Official:
T. W. C. MOORE, A. A. G.

HEADQUARTERS MILITARY DIVISION OF THE GULF,
OFFICE OF THE CHIEF SIGNAL OFFICER,
NEW ORLEANS, LA., November 18, 1865.

Major-General P. H. Sheridan, U. S. Army:

GENERAL—I have the honor to report that the number of Confederate prisoners received by the forces under your command from August first, 1864, to March first, 1865, was about thirteen thousand. The names of nearly that number are recorded on the books recently used in the office of the Provost-Marshal General, Middle Military Division.

Respectfully submitted,

E. B. PARSONS,
Late Provost-Marshal General,
Middle Military Division.

Official:
T. W. C. MOORE,
Assistant Adjutant-General.

www.ingramcontent.com/pod-product-compliance
Lightning Source LLC
LaVergne TN
LVHW011218110826
845150LV00006B/1464